General editor: Graham Handley MA Ph.D.

Brodie's Notes on William Golding's
The ~~~~~~~~~~~ World

Graham Handley

M 150th YEAR
MACMILLAN

© Graham Handley 1979

All rights reserved. No reproduction, copy or transmission of
this publication may be made without written permission.

No paragraph of this publication may be reproduced, copied or
transmitted save with written permission or in accordance with
the provisions of the Copyright, Designs and Patents Act 1988,
or under the terms of any licence permitting limited copying
issued by the Copyright Licensing Agency, 90 Tottenham Court
Road, London W1P 9HE.

Any person who does any unauthorised act in relation to this
publication may be liable to criminal prosecution and civil
claims for damages.

First published 1979 by Pan Books Ltd

This revised edition published 1993 by
THE MACMILLAN PRESS LTD
Houndmills, Basingstoke, Hampshire RG21 2XS
and London
Companies and representatives
throughout the world

ISBN 0-333-59744-3

Typeset by Footnote Graphics, Warminster, Wiltshire
Printed in Great Britain by
Cox & Wyman Ltd, Reading

Contents

Preface by the general editor 5

The author and his work 7

17th-century background 11

The Restoration Theatre 15

Plot summary 21

Act summaries, critical commentary, textual notes and revision questions 22

The characters 71
Millament 71
Mirabell 73
Fainall 75
Mrs Marwood 76
Lady Wishfort 78
Witwoud 79
Petulant 80
Sir Wilfull Witwoud 81
Other characters 81

Structure and style 83
Structure 83
Style 83

General questions and sample answer in note form 89

Further reading 91

Preface

The intention throughout this study aid is to stimulate and guide, to encourage your involvement in the book, and to develop informed responses and a sure understanding of the main details.

Brodie's Notes provide a clear outline of the play or novel's plot, followed by act, scene, or chapter summaries and/or commentaries. These are designed to emphasize the most important literary and factual details. Poems, stories or non-fiction texts combine brief summary with critical commentary on individual aspects or common features of the genre being examined. Textual notes define what is difficult or obscure and emphasize literary qualities. Revision questions are set at appropriate points to test your ability to appreciate the prescribed book and to write accurately and relevantly about it.

In addition, each of these Notes includes a critical appreciation of the author's art. This covers such major elements as characterization, style, structure, setting and themes. Poems are examined technically – rhyme, rhythm, for instance. In fact, any important aspect of the prescribed work will be evaluated. The aim is to send you back to the text you are studying.

Each study aid concludes with a series of general questions which require a detailed knowledge of the book: some of these questions may invite comparison with other books, some will be suitable for coursework exercises, and some could be adapted to work you are doing on another book or books. Each study aid has been adapted to meet the needs of the current examination requirements. They provide a basic, individual and imaginative response to the work being studied, and it is hoped that they will stimulate you to acquire disciplined reading habits and critical fluency.

Graham Handley 1990

A close reading of the play is the student's primary task. These Notes will help to increase your understanding and appreciation of the play, and to stimulate *your own* thinking about it: *they are in no way intended as a substitute* for a thorough knowledge of the play.

Page references in these Notes are to the Penguin edition of *Four English Comedies*, edited by J. M. Morrell; but as references are also made to each act, the Notes may be used with any edition of the play.

The author and his work

William Congreve was born at Bardsley, near Leeds, in 1670. His father, an army officer, was posted to Ireland in 1674, and William was sent to a school in Kilkenny, where one of his senior schoolfellows was Jonathan Swift. At the age of sixteen Congreve, who had already shown literary talent and cultural interests, was entered at Trinity College, Dublin, where he continued his friendship with Swift. In 1688 the Congreves returned to England, staying at the family seat, Stretton Hall in Staffordshire. Meanwhile Congreve attended the Middle Temple in London, though he never applied any real sense of discipline to his legal studies, and was able to move freely in the literary and society circles of his time. His first play was *The Old Bachelor*, which was later carefully gone over by John Dryden (1631–1700), but in 1692 Congreve published a novel, *Incognita*. Critics have found much in this to link it with the later plays, but it appears to be merely a somewhat conventional exercise in Romantic escapism in the pre-Gothic period. The scene is Florence, and here is a fair example of the kind of language employed in dialogue:

'If I do not usurp a priviledge reserved for some one more happy in your acquaintance, may I presume, Madam, to entreat (for a while) the favour of your conversation, at least till the arrival of who you expect, provided you are not tired of me before; for then upon the least intimation of uneasiness, I will not fail of doing my self the violence to withdraw for your release.'

This is from Aurelian, the hero; but the theme, romantically explored, involves mistaken identity, with the inevitable 'all's well that ends well'. The language is refined, exaggerated, full of the hyperboles of good breeding and romantic expression, exquisitely balanced and fashioned at best, boringly predictable for the most part. It is unrelieved by humour, and nowhere approaches realism, so that the result is artificial, removed from life. The same could be said, of course, of much Restoration comedy, but it generally has the compensation of wit and the mirror of morality to enhance it.

Congreve wrote poetry and produced delicate translations from the classics in the 1690s; from Dryden (himself engaged in translation), Congreve received practical advice, assistance and friendship. The polishing of *The Old Bachelor* made for its success when it was produced at the Theatre Royal in 1693, and Congreve was fortunate not only in having literary help but also the presence in the cast of the fine actress Anne Bracegirdle. The play ran for fourteen performances – quite a feat in those days – and the young man was hailed as the natural heir to the old poet who had helped him so much, and who had acclaimed him critically.

Congreve was not slow to take advantage of his success, and another comedy, *The Double-Dealer*, was in production before the end of 1693. It was not successful, despite some laudatory verses from Dryden appended to the printed version of the play. In 1695 Congreve returned to favour with *Love for Love*, acted by a new company of which he became the manager; the new company included Mrs Bracegirdle and many of the other best actors and actresses of the time. Congreve changed his direction somewhat with his next play, a tragedy called *The Mourning Bride* which was produced in 1697 and was a financial success. He continued to produce odes and verses in the manner of the time; while not distinguished, they show that tendency towards refinement, polish and balance that is the hallmark of the equally highly polished dialogue of his final play. He also wrote an important essay concerning 'Humour in Comedy', which defines the underlying seriousness of his own art; but after that he essayed a reply to *A Short View of the Immorality and Profaneness of the English Stage (1699)*, by Jeremy Collier (1650–1726), which did little to enhance his own reputation or his capacity for debate. By the time *The Way of the World* was performed in 1700, the comedy of wit was experiencing a popular decline; and Congreve at the age of thirty turned his back upon the stage he had just graced with his most exquisite comedy. William Hazlitt (1778–1830) wrote these words as a tribute to the unique nature of Congreve's achievement:

He had by far the most wit and elegance, with less of other things, of humour, character, incident, etc. His style is inimitable, nay perfect. It is the highest model of comic dialogue. Every sentence is replete with sense and satire, conveyed in the most polished and pointed terms. Every page represents a shower of brilliant conceits, is a tissue of epigrams in prose, is a new triumph of wit, a new conquest over dullness. The fire of artful raillery is nowhere else so well kept up. (William Hazlitt, *Lectures on the English Comic Writers*, 1819)

After *The Way of the World* Congreve worked in a somewhat desultory fashion at Lincoln's Inn Fields; wrote a masque; went into a managerial partnership with his fellow dramatist Vanbrugh, but gave that up after an unsuccessful season. He began to withdraw, did not wish to make new friends, and certainly experienced by the comparatively young age of thirty-five a lassitude towards the theatre and, indeed, towards life. He was however, intimate with Mrs Bracegirdle, and continued to attend plays in which she appeared, though after about ten years their relationship appeared to be in decline. Financially things were not good, though various government positions came Congreve's way. In 1705, however, he was left £1,000; he gave up the post of Commissioner for licensing hackney coaches and became Commissioner for wine licenses, which brought him in a salary of £100 per annum. Despite a change of government in 1710, Congreve held on to his post; and in 1714 he became Under-Searcher for Customs in the Pool of London as well as Secretary for Jamaica. He was comparatively wealthy for the rest of his life.

By 1710, when his works were published in three volumes, Congreve's health had deteriorated: he was nearly blind, and suffered acutely from gout; nevertheless he remained cheerful. In 1725 he made a will in which he left his effects to the Second Duchess of Marlborough, who was his closest friend in these declining years. (He may have been the father of her younger daughter.) In 1726 he was visited by Voltaire, but deprecated his own literary achievement, valuing himself, so he said, more as a gentleman than as a writer. His final years were marred by ill health, and he died in 1729; he is buried in Westminster Abbey. Pope, who was of the next generation, valued him so highly that he dedicated his translation of the *Iliad* to him, but in the nineteenth century there was a considerable reaction against him and against Restoration comedy generally. Here two critics in particular deserve a closer look. First, William Makepeace Thackeray (1811–63), in *The English Humourists of the Eighteenth Century* (1851):

> The Congreve Muse is dead, and her song choked in Time's ashes. We gaze at the skeleton, and wonder at the life which once revelled in its mad veins. We take the skull up, and muse over the frolic and daring, the wit, scorn, passion, hope, desire, with which that empty bowl was once fermented. What does it mean? the measures, the grimaces, the bowing, shuffling and retreating. It has a jargon of its own, quite unlike life; a sort of moral of its own quite unlike life too.

Thomas Babington Macaulay (1800–59) in his masterly essay on *The Comic Dramatists of the Restoration*, tempers justice with disapproval in the fine balance of his own summing up:

> Wycherley had some knowledge of books; but Congreve was a man of real learning. Congreve's offences against decorum, though highly culpable, were not so gross as those of Wycherley; nor did Congreve, like Wycherley, exhibit to the world the deplorable spectacle of licentious dotage.

The debate about the merits and demerits of Restoration comedy, often with particular reference to the two dramatists named above, has continued into our own time. Such distinguished critics as L. C. Knights (*Restoration Comedy: the Reality and the Myth*) and F. W. Bateson (*Essays in Critical Dissent*) represent the extremes of the critical spectrum. Is Restoration comedy moral? amoral? immoral? Is it great literature, dated literature, dead literature; rooted in its time or for all time? The controversy will go on, for the phases of drama are as shifting and changing as the phases of popular music. The literary historian must evaluate, despite the taste of his own time. Today's reader of Congreve must prepare to make an imaginative leap, in order to appreciate a society in many ways unlike our own, and yet having recognizable points of contact with it. *The Way of the World* may appear dead to us as it did to Thackeray; in forty years' time a play like *Rosencrantz and Guildenstern are Dead* may seem the aberration of a decadent culture. The only way to make the leap successfully is to read with the eye of the imagination, and with an awareness of and a respect for, the conventions of the time.

17th-century background

The Stuart monarchy was restored in 1660 after nearly twenty years of Commonwealth rule that ended with the death of Oliver Cromwell (1599–1658), the Lord Protector. This meant largely a return to the era of the 1630s in terms of Church affairs; the Dissenters who had triumphed now found themselves in opposition to the resuscitated Anglicans. With Charles II came the Court, with its strong French influence, and Parliament once more bore allegiance to the King instead of being elevated to a power of its own. Thus, the divisions of society that had existed before the Civil War still prevailed: Cavaliers encountered Puritans; and the aristocracy found themselves separated from the merchant classes by interests and status. By 1679 the High Church and the aristocracy were instrumental in forming the Tory party, just as the Dissenters and trade factions largely supported the Whigs.

Apart from the drama, the period of unrest gave rise to some distinguished prose and poetry which reflected the divisions of the day. Important evidence of the society life of the times is provided by the *Diary* of Samuel Pepys (1633–1703). Pepys was at Magdalene College, Cambridge, during the years of the Commonwealth, but adapted his views and habits to the demands of the changed times after the restoration of the monarchy. His diary has been described as 'a historical source-book for the facts, anecdotes, scandals and atmosphere of the period'. He was on the fringe of the Court and, though somewhat culpable himself, frequently deplored its excesses.

English writers of the time looked back to the pre-Commonwealth period and the classicism of Ben Jonson. In verse the ideal was an amalgam of balance, elevation and rational treatment – exemplified in *Cooper's Hill* (written as early as 1642), by Sir John Denham (1615–69) – with its ease, harmony and skilled use of the heroic couplet. This emphasis on elegance and correctness was itself a reaction against metaphysical modes of hyperbole, intellectual ingenuity and strained wit – as distinct from the 'easy' writing of Suckling praised by Millamant in *The Way of the World*. The movement is towards the couplet, initiated by Dryden (1631–1700), and later adopted by Pope.

The 'world' was the world of society and politics, and Dryden's *Absalom and Achitophel* (1681) heralded the arrival of political satire with a vengeance; the biblical allegory is in fact a broadside, aimed in particular at the Whigs and the Earl of Shaftesbury. Dryden speaks for the age and is the master of its many modes: comedy, tragedy, satire, lyrics, odes, translations, adaptations – all these flow from his pen. In addition we must note his rational examination of critical theory. He is the literary lawgiver of the period, ruling the town from the coffee-house and the study. In 1670 he was appointed Poet Laureate, and in 1678 he rewrote Shakespeare's *Antony and Cleopatra* to fit the literary convention of the times, calling it *All for Love*. His poem *Religio Laici* (1682) indicated his concern to 'explain' religion, which ultimately led to his being converted to Catholicism. He defended his changed faith in *The Hind and the Panther* (1687), for his conversion had been interpreted by many as mercenary, since James II (a Catholic) had succeeded to the throne in 1685 on the death of Charles II. In his last years Dryden produced translations of the Roman satirists and issued his *Fables* (1700), which were chiefly adaptations from Chaucer and Boccaccio. None of these works showed any evidence of declining powers.

We should here consider the intellectual temper of the age, dominated as it was by the spirit and precepts of rationalism. The movement generally was away from superstition (belief in witchcraft, for example), and towards the scientific spirit that inevitably undermined religious orthodoxy. Thomas Hobbes (1588–1679) and John Locke (1632–1704) were the great philosophers of the time. Hobbes, in his *Leviathan* (1651) presented a cynical, materialistic view of society, with the state the all-powerful preserver of order and peace among men. There was no place for love nor for its elevated manifestation, idealism. Hobbes was vigorously attacked on all levels, from Dissent to Orthodoxy.

Locke's *Two Treatises of Government* (1689), posited the theory that government exists, or is based on, a contract between the governed and those who govern. (In religion, too, there was some emphasis on rationalism; a belief in natural religion or deism arose, and the orthodox brought some rational scrutiny to bear on the authority of scripture.) Locke's *Essay concerning Human Understanding* (1690) comes to the conclusion that experience provides the ultimate in knowledge of which the mind is capable. Obviously this is a sceptical view, as later philosophers were quick to demonstrate, yet the rational scientific emphasis is evident.

In the post-Restoration period the Dissenters lived under legal restrictions and penalties, but one writer from their ranks stands out, as far removed from the Restoration Court and its plays as anyone could possibly be. John Bunyan (1628–88) was born in Bedford, of humble stock; he served in the Parliamentary army and, after the Restoration, wrote his autobiography *Grace Abounding to the Chief of Sinners* (1666). He became a dissenting preacher, was imprisoned for some years for preaching without a licence, and in 1678 wrote the first part of *The Pilgrim's Progress*. His was the religion of personal illumination, a current running across the times. His great book transcended the narrow limitations of sect and place, its allegory becoming the recognizable symbol for Christian behaviour, of fallen human nature beset by temptation but triumphing in the end. It reached the common people as the novels of Dickens were to reach them just over a century and a half later, but it took a long time to penetrate the reaches of a society whose religion was dependent on the dogmas of orthodoxy.

The novel as an art form had not yet arrived, and the prose of the period is distinguished by the Earl of Clarendon's *True Historical Narrative of the Rebellion and Civil Wars in England* (1704–7); Thomas Sprat wrote his *History of the Royal Society* (1667), and that Society took a special interest in the improvement of its written papers in terms of the language used. The Society also set up a committee, which included Dryden, to facilitate improvements in prose writing; later, Dr Samuel Johnson (1709–84) was to praise Dryden's contribution, declaring that he was responsible for teaching writers 'to think naturally and write forcibly'. Political writing is seen at its best in the Marquis of Halifax's essays, those of Sir William

Temple, and Halifax's *The Character of a Trimmer* (1685); these set a pattern of literary taste which was to last well into the next century.

Dryden died in 1700 and, in effect, an age had passed away. The drama was to become rather more tame; classicism and rationalism were to be further developed and explored in Pope, Addison and Steele. Periodical literature was to become established, with the giant Dr Johnson presiding over taste. The major change in the early to mid eighteenth century is the evolution of the novel as a serious art form: for example, the vast and heterogeneous output of Daniel Defoe (1660–1731) included *Robinson Crusoe* (1720) and *Moll Flanders* (1722); *Gulliver's Travels* by Jonathan Swift (1667–1745) followed in 1726. By the middle of the century these would have given way to the moral measures of *Pamela* (1740) by Samuel Richardson (1689–1761), and to the ebullience and zest of *Tom Jones* (1749) by Henry Fielding (1707–54).

The Restoration Theatre

It was in November 1660 that two companies of actors known as the King's and the Duke's (after Charles II and the Duke of York) were formed. The King's Company eventually moved to the Theatre Royal – later to become Drury Lane – and Pepys the diarist was one of the first to see a play there after its opening on 7 May 1663. The first theatre held about five hundred people and the stage, covered in green baize, projected into the pit. Wax candles provided the lighting until, later, oil lamps were used as footlights. Three sides of the theatre had boxes; above them were the middle galleries, and above those the upper ones. During the Great Plague the theatres were closed from June 1665 until November 1666; in 1669 the Duke's Theatre in Dorset Garden, overlooking the Thames, was built. On 25 January 1672 the Theatre Royal was destroyed by fire; Christopher Wren was commissioned to design the new Theatre Royal in Bridges Street; it was completed at a cost exceeding £4,000, and opened in 1674. There was a virtual merger of the two companies in 1682, with the Dorset Garden Theatre presenting operas and spectacular plays in the main, while those not requiring special effects were produced at the Theatre Royal.

Most of the plays were performed in contemporary dress: periwigs, wide-brimmed hats, long coats and lace cravats for the men: and gowns after the French fashion, displaying the neck and a generous expanse of cleavage, for the actresses. The tiring rooms contained a variety of costumes, some of them gifts from the King or the aristocracy. The players were under the authority – and protection – of the Lord Chamberlain; some had shares in the company, others were merely hired actors with no secure employment. Part of the reaction against the years of Puritan rule was seen in the fact that women now appeared on the English stage, replacing the boy players who had, for example, played the Shakespearean heroines from the 1590s onwards. This gave an immediate lift to the theatre, and it must be said that many of the actors and actresses were respectable and took a great pride in their art.

Many of the hireling players however, were debauched and licentious, drunkenness on stage being quite common: there was fine acting and there was mediocrity. The theatres were open for about forty weeks of the year; they could be closed temporarily for the death of a nobleman, and the actors obviously needed both stamina and resilience, since plays often ran for a short time only and were frequently changed.

The court, the wealthy and fashionable, and many holding small appointments, formed the mainstay of the audiences; apprentices and servants provided the lower social levels. The King could make or ruin a playwright (they were called 'poets' in the language of the time) by his comments on a play; and the audience usually took their cue from his reaction. These audiences were almost exclusively of Anglican and Royalist sympathy. With the rise of the political parties, the Tories and the Whigs, the former controlled the playhouses until 1689, when the Whigs were in the ascendant following the invitation to William and Mary to come over from Holland and rule England. The playgoers provide a curious paradox: many of them would attend balls and masques; but they would also exult in the public spectacle of the hanging, drawing and quartering of a condemned man at Tyburn, or the burning alive of a woman at Smithfield. Bull-baiting and cockfighting were their sports, and the theatres witnessed brawls and fights that gave rise to duels; on occasions there was death within the theatres themselves. Frequently the pit was occupied by drunken youths intent on violence, not far removed, perhaps, from some of today's football supporters at matches.

The playwrights obviously wrote with a shrewd knowledge of the acting strengths of the company – and from 1682 until 1695 only one company existed. 'The poet's performance' was the third day's net profits, which meant he might get £100 or so if he were lucky. The professional playwright was in competition with 'gentlemen' amateurs, who wrote, or affected to write, for pleasure only. But some professionals had the compensation of aristocratic patronage, hence the fulsome dedications before some of the plays. Satire was the order of the day, though it was rarely directed against the aristocracy whose power was such that they could swiftly terminate the run of a play if it was not to their taste. Allied to this was the emphasis on 'wit', which meant placing a premium not on what was said but on the manner of saying it. 'Wit' was interpreted variously: to the bullies it might embody a practical joke; to the courtiers its boundaries were measured by brilliant repartee, by the use of the double entendre, or by barbs of verbal malice. The intellectual wit could fashion an epigram, distil his wisdom into an antithesis, or philosophize; the playwright needed to be acutely aware of these various ironic modes, and adept at using them. Later the poet Alexander Pope (1688–1744) was to give his own definition of wit:

> True wit is Nature to advantage dressed,
> What oft was thought, but ne'er so well expressed.

By the standards of Restoration Comedy, this definition has strict and unacceptable limitations; Dryden, the foremost dramatist of the time, preferred to think that wit depended exclusively on imaginative ingenuity.

Space precludes anything like a full treatment of Restoration tragedy, which shared the scene equally with comedy at that time. As John Harold Wilson observes in Chapter 11 of *A Preface to Restoration Drama* (see *Further reading*), 'Comedy was the Restoration's finest dramatic flower, yet few contemporary critics found occasion to admire its gaudy blossoms.' Be that as it may, comedy has stood the test of critical time rather better than its respected competitor. Comedy was written in prose, and this was one of the contemporary objections to it; moreover, it was generally thought that comedy should have a function that, in the words of Jeremy Collier, was 'to recommend virtue and discountenance vice'.

Certainly Restoration Comedy has lewdness and sexual licence at the forefront of its themes, a reflection of the mood of the times and a natural reaction against the confines of Puritanism. George Farquhar (c.1677–1707), among others, affected to take the view that he and his fellow dramatists intended to reform morals, asserting, 'To make the moral instructive, you must make the play diverting'. Dryden, on the other hand, considered that it was 'the business of the poet . . . to make you laugh'. Wilson argues persuasively that Restoration

Comedy has been unfairly abused, particularly by the Victorians, who, while admitting its wit and polish (though tending to stigmatize the latter as artificiality), disliked its rational and free approach to sex.

The first Restoration dramatists followed their masters of the pre-Puritan period. Dryden caught the mood and morality of the times when he revised *The Wild Gallant* in 1667, and Wilson describes this new mode succinctly when he says that it was 'characterized by brisk dialogue, cynical and sexual wit, libertine gentlemen, and emancipated ladies'. In addition, there was often an anti-marriage theme or situation (this was to become a dramatic convention of the time); adultery was the stock-in-trade; and abnormally lustful older women were frequently present. The comedy took a number of definable forms: farce; burlesque; satire; 'humours' comedy; and, at the highest and most refined level, the comedy of wit. Here we are concerned mainly with the latter, but across these *genres*, the themes of cuckolding, deception, and libertine activities are common. A celebrated burlesque of *The Tempest* (in part written by Dryden) was successful, as indeed were the burlesque comedies of Farquhar.

Some playwrights turned back to and adapted the 'humours of Ben Jonson' (Jonson had given to each of his comic characters one leading trait, called a 'humour'). Medieval physiologists had asserted that a man's character was dependent on the four fluids (humours) present in his body. These were blood, black bile, yellow bile and phlegm – separately approximating to the sanguine, melancholy, choleric or phlegmatic parts of nature. These 'humours' were believed to be closely related to the emotions, hence a preponderance of one could disturb the balance of the character. In the Restoration period this tendency was somewhat debased, but Thomas Shadwell (c.1642–92) and Dryden in their different ways re-established the 'humours' theory, Shadwell by a narrow adherence to the ideas of Jonson, Dryden through the more liberal view that character could consist of a 'miscellany of humours'. William Wycherley (c. 1640–1716) extended the 'humours' concept, attacked pretenders and hypocrites, and was sceptical of both religion and morality. *The Country Wife* (1675) is his most justly celebrated comedy, with Horner as his natural man gaining access to the ladies of the town by affecting to be impotent as a result of having the 'pox' (venereal disease) which seems to have had a fascination – perhaps because it was so widespread – for the hedonistic society of the Reformation. The notorious 'china' scene in which Horner 'has' Lady Fidget until he can 'have' her no more, is a brilliantly sustained situation, with Sir Jasper assisting at his own cuckolding. Wycherley was obviously influenced by the French dramatist Molière, whose attack on the ramifications of hypocrisy preceded his own.

From Wycherley to Congreve is a leap from a galaxy of comic effects to the refined distillation of wit. The latter may involve word-play, epigrams, asides – many ways of linking the unexpected and the dissimilar in terms of seeming or real wisdom. It deals with the world of fashion, and is thus sophisticated, intellectual, subtle, yet with judgement and discretion in its terms of reference. By 1676, with *The Man of Mode* by Sir George Etherege (1635–92), the comedy of wit had arrived; and *The Way of the World*, though too late for the taste of the time, represents its most distinguished level.

Plot summary

The student is advised first to read through *The Way of the World* twice or more – without attempting detailed work on the text at that stage – in order to grasp at least the outline of what is a complex plot. Certainly every opportunity should be taken to see the play if possible – though it is seldom revived – but it should be read beforehand: while watching a performance one is carried forward and has no chance to look back. Read, therefore, and concentrate on *knowing* the plot; if you absorb its details, you will the more readily understand the motivations of the characters.

The relationship of Lady Wishfort to the other characters is crucial to a full understanding of the play. She is a widow and her two sisters are dead; one of these sisters was the mother of Millamant, but the latter will receive only half her inheritance if she marries without her aunt's (Lady Wishfort's) consent. Naturally, if her choice is approved by Lady Wishfort, she comes into her full fortune. Here the complications begin. Mirabell, who loves Millamant, has paid court to Lady Wishfort, but the insincerity of that courtship (undertaken as a cover for his love for Millamant) has been revealed to Lady Wishfort by her 'friend' Mrs Marwood, who, though mistress to Fainall, is herself attracted by Mirabell. Lady Wishfort is naturally angry, and thus unlikely to agree to a match between her niece Millamant and her own ex-suitor Mirabell. But Lady Wishfort's other deceased sister was the mother of Sir Wilfull Witwoud; after her death her husband married again and sired a son, Anthony Witwoud, who is thus half-brother to Sir Wilfull. Lady Wishfort herself has a daughter, Mrs Fainall, whose first marriage was to one Languish, who has died; her second to Fainall, who converts her fortune.

Here the plot divides into two separate strands. The first has Mirabell, intent on winning Millamant, seeking to compromise Lady Wishfort by passing off his servant Waitwell as his fictitious uncle, Sir Rowland. As Waitwell has just married Foible, Lady Wishfort's maid, Mirabell is confident that Lady Wishfort will consent to his own marriage to Millamant as the price of his silence on Lady Wishfort's false marriage to 'Sir Rowland'. The design fails.

The second strand involves Fainall, who seeks to discredit his wife (who has previously had an affair with Mirabell) to her mother. In this he is aided and abetted by his mistress, Mrs Marwood, their aim being Lady Wishfort's fortune as the price of *their* silence. Intrigue and deception follow, revelation succeeds revelation, but ultimately Mirabell triumphs. He and Millamant, mainly in Act 4, make clear their love for each other, and afterwards Mirabell enlists the aid of Sir Wilfull Witwoud in their plot. Mrs Fainall, armed with Foible's evidence of her husband's infidelity with Mrs Marwood, decides to denounce him to her mother and thus counter his scheme. Mirabell at the same time affects to renounce Millamant to Sir Wilfull, but when Fainall tries to effect the final blackmail, his wife and Mirabell reveal, via Waitwell's black box of papers, that Mrs Fainall, suspicious of Fainall's motives, had, before her marriage, made a deed of conveyance of her estate in favour of Mirabell. She now holds the whip hand, thereby giving her union with her errant husband some hope of success. Mirabell, having saved Lady Wishfort's fortune and her reputation, can now claim Millamant with her aunt's blessing.

In the final reckoning, the way of the world is perhaps not redolent of Fainall's cynicism but of the rightness of feeling that seeks to save a marriage rather than wreck it; and which, in the case of Mirabell and Millamant, undertakes a marriage based on mutual respect and recognition of faults and independence, and a knowledge of the falsehoods of fashion and fortune.

Act summaries, critical commentary, textual notes and revision questions

The text used for the following is that given in *Four English Comedies* (edited by J. M. Morrell) in the Penguin Plays edition. The four plays are *Volpone, She Stoops to Conquer, The School for Scandal*, and *The Way of the World* (pp.131–231).

There are no notes in the Penguin text, but the editor has indicated a number of arbitrary scene divisions which do not correspond with other editors' texts of the play. *These scene divisions are therefore put in brackets (thus (Act 1, Scene 7) to indicate the Penguin text, but **Act** summaries are given throughout to avoid confusion*. Other texts used here in conjunction with the Penguin text are:
Congreve: Incognita and the Way of the World, edited by A. Norman Jeffares, (Arnold's English Texts); an excellent edition with good notes and fine critical introduction. *Congreve: The Way of the World*, edited by Kathleen M. Lynch, (Regents Restoration Drama Series). Competent edition and notes.

Prologue

This was spoken by Thomas Betterton, one of the leading actors of the day. It is written in heroic couplets (i.e. two lines rhyming together) with the occasional variation of the triplet. The couplet was the accepted mode of verse composition at the time, and Congreve here reveals his lip-service to the convention, and his mastery of it. The body of the play is written in prose, but Restoration tragedy was often written in blank verse or rhyme: the latter being employed, for example, in Dryden's *The Conquest of Granada* (1669–70). The prologue, and indeed the epilogue, were important parts of the convention, indicating themes, providing comments, and attacking (or defending) a particular aspect of society.

Here the Prologue establishes in the first few lines the fact that poets (playwrights) fare worse in life than fools do; poets obtain a brief success in town, but every undertaking is a gamble. The author realizes that he cannot rest on his past achievements, for he may find that in this play he has forfeited his claims to success. Though what he has written has cost him much labour, he begs to be condemned if his play is dull; he claims to have plot, 'new thought' and humour, but no farce or satire (though this is obviously said with tongue in cheek, for he affects to believe that the town is 'reform'd' and that there is therefore no need for his satirical shafts). Of course, he may also be commenting on the change in taste and the decline of comedy, particularly the comedy of wit. He asserts that he merely wishes to entertain, to expose fools occasionally (though there obviously won't be any in the audience!); he gives himself up entirely to the judgement of this audience.

Note the perfect balance of the rhyming couplets, which anticipate the rational balance – the true wit – of the play. That Congreve is laughing at his audience there can be little doubt. He is registering current standards, making modest claims for himself, but adopting a defensive stance, as was customary. At the same time we feel that, patronage apart, he couldn't care less – he knows his own worth and particularly his own aims.

ill stars i.e. misfortune.
fools ... fortune ... fools ... forsakes Note the alliterative run and word-play in these carefully balanced couplets.
oafs i.e. stupid people.
the cuckoo-eggs A reference to the practice of the cuckoo, which lays its eggs in another bird's nest.
portion ... dotes i.e. share ... spoils.
bubbles Fools (carrying on the association of the previous lines).
drawn in i.e. lured, attracted.
Suffer'd i.e. allowed.
stakes ... hazards Notice that the language echoes the gambling of the time which would be common in society – this is almost a casual moral comment.
butter'd Flattered, fawned upon.
undone Ruined (generally, financially).
Parnassus This was the mountain in Greece that was the home of the Nine Muses, the inspirers of poetry, music and the allied arts.
on mature deliberation i.e. (dullness) is all the more inexcusable after much thought has produced it.

hiss'd-off By the audience in the theatre.
For so reform'd a town An ironic look perhaps at the effects produced by Jeremy Collier's *A Short View of the English Stage* (1698).
a passive poet Heavy irony – the audience can make of the play what they will.

Act 1

Mirabell and Fainall, two men of fashion, are playing cards in a Chocolate-House. The conversation is immediately free, with Fainall twitting and mocking Mirabell over his interest in Mrs Millamant, and at the same time finding out what has happened on the previous night. Mirabell had in fact left the company that contained Millamant's two followers, Witwoud and Petulant, Mrs Marwood (Fainall's mistress), Mrs Fainall – and Lady Wishfort, to whom Mirabell once paid sham court. After further conversation about the 'Cabal-nights' where the above-named 'sit upon the murdered reputations of the week', Fainall goes off and a servant brings news to Mirabell that his man Waitwell has married (Foible, Lady Wishfort's maid) in accordance with Mirabell's scheme; with the return of Fainall, Mirabell reveals that he has a scheme 'which is not yet ripe for discovery' and they further discuss Mirabell's interest in Millamant. The next entrance brings a messenger from Sir Wilfull Witwoud for his half-brother, who attends on Millamant; Fainall and Mirabell discuss this country-cousin, who is coming to town to 'equip himself for travel'. It must be remembered that Sir Wilfull is Lady Wishfort's nephew. Witwoud next appears, pitying himself (a man of fashion!) for having to entertain this unwelcome half-brother, and talks exhaustively about the lack of talent (or wit) in his 'friend' Petulant. A servant then reports that three gentlewomen are waiting outside in a coach for Petulant, and this occasions further ribald comment; Witwoud maintains that this is all an act on Petulant's part, and that he has probably deliberately arranged for them to call in order to create an impression. Petulant, when he appears, refuses to go out to them, and they are reported to have left in anger. Petulant further reveals that he has heard that an uncle of

Mirabell's has come to town, and may if he marries do him out of his inheritance. Witwoud repeats much the same story to Fainall, and thinks that perhaps the Uncle will court Millamant and thus displace Mirabell there too. Petulant and Witwoud, Mirabell and Fainall, then make their separate ways to the Mall.

The presentation is of the public world: these are gentlemen at ease and leisure, indulging themselves, having nothing better to do. Notice that they are gambling for money, and that money is perhaps the major theme of the play. Fainall sounds another theme, that of the sex war, with a play on 'play'. Mirabell immediately shows his own sarcastic wit, Fainall his probing propensity. There is too an indication of the claustrophobic closeness of family relationships ('her aunt, your wife's mother'). Already Mirabell's submerged feelings for Millamant are being shown between the lines, and the details of the plot – and the past plot – are revealed by the conversation. Mirabell's account of his courtship of Lady Wishfort underlines the morality, the way, of this superficial world. Both men are aware of the need to test each other out, and both react accordingly. Mirabell's praise of Millamant is not merely for effect: in fact we feel or sense the sincerity of it: 'They are now grown as familiar to me as my own frailties' is a self-acknowledgment, for in his mind (and heart) there is the wish to 'share' everything with her. The account of Sir Wilfull is again emphatic of the closeness of family relationships, while the entrance of his brother after this is dramatically, almost ridiculously, effective. The play on 'half' (with the implication of half wit), the emphasis on memory, the levels of superficial exchange, all these emphasize the ironic/satirical edge with which Congreve is contemplating his creatures, and of course exposing them. True wits reveal the limitations of false ones, and Witwoud, intent on proving his own wit, puts his friend Petulant down. We ask ourselves if people of this kind can possibly possess any qualities of sincerity: they appear to live only in the image which they are intent on presenting to the world. Fashion and affectation are all. Mirabell and Fainall delight in fooling Witwoud – in a way their verbal accomplishment is an extension of their 'play'. Wit is a game, lack of wit a measure of failure. Witwoud delights in exposing

Petulant's reputation by his coarse innuendo about the strumpets and the bawd, emphasizing that the women are paid to appear: the game of scoring off your friends is being played at various levels. Witwoud expatiates on the devices to attract attention which Petulant employs, and this provides further evidence (whether true or false) of the superficiality – the image reputation – by which society lives. These masks cover a sordid reality. The plot is established by direct reference to the uncle, and then Mirabell further and brilliantly indulges his wit at the expense of Petulant, though the latter gets some revenge through his remarks which put down Witwoud. The latter may secretly admire, and envy, Petulant, whose social qualities are criticized by Mirabell.

(Act 1, Scene 1)

A Chocolate-House i.e. where chocolate is served (as a drink), the resort of fashionable men.
gamester Gambler.
a woman who undervalued the loss of her reputation i.e. one who did not enjoy losing her reputation by having an affair. This is the first of the moral reversals of the play.
delicate ... are for refining on your pleasures Mirabell is being sarcastic at Fainall's affectation.
grave ... gay Notice the simple use of antithesis, the latter being a marked feature of the word-play in *The Way of the World*.
humours i.e. given to moods.
a Stoic A person of great self-control, showing indifference to pleasure or pain.
coxcomb A fop, vain and foolish.
Witwoud and Petulant Note the names, which indicate the main bias in the character of each – he who would be thought a wit and one given to cavilling and pettiness.
Lady Wishfort Again the pun in the name, the sexual 'wish for it'; or the meaning could be 'strong wish'.
a lasting passion i.e. a strong dislike (because he has affected to pay court to her).
grave faces They pretended to be serious.
the vapours An almost fashionable complaint – it really means faintness and depression.
I would not have understood her i.e. I would have pretended not to notice what she said.
reddened i.e. blushed.

in compliance with her aunt In agreeing with her aunt's expressed opinion.

such a resignation Having to give herself up to (another's views). The comment implies Millamant's independence.

half her fortune ... my lady's approbation Half her inheritance depends on Lady Wishfort's consent (to her marriage), an important plot note.

Cabal-nights A cabal is a clique (from the French *cabale*). In England the word came into common usage in the reign of Charles II, as it was a contraction of the first letter in the name of each member of the small but powerful 'Committee for Foreign Affairs' responsible directly to Charles (Clifford, Arlington, Buckingham, Ashley and Lauderdale).

like the coroner's inquest ... murdered reputations A fine witty image to indicate the obsession with gossip and scandal that was the mark of fashionable society at the time – or perhaps an even wider comment on human nature and its delight in damning others.

one man ... Witwoud and Petulant were enrolled members Note the irony here: two men of this kind (followers, fashionable 'wits') are only equivalent to one real man.

foundress ... sect A faked religious tone to underline Mirabell's irony.

ratafia An almond-flavoured liqueur. The implication is that Lady Wishfort speaks of merely taking a liqueur with a friend, but is really lustful.

shift for itself i.e. make its own arrangements.

separation i.e. this division (between you).

dissembled better i.e. lied more successfully.

guilty of a song in her commendation i.e. I so demeaned myself that I wrote her a poem (Congreve's own irony at the expense of those who 'drop into verse' is apparent).

a lampoon i.e. a virulent satire.

an affair with a young fellow i.e. Mirabell says he was giving her a 'reputation' (which was flattering to one of her age).

carried so far i.e. made so much of.

of a dropsy i.e. suffering from an excess of fluid in the body tissues.

The devil's in't i.e. one would have to enlist the aid of the devil.

my virtue forbade me Mirabell is being 'delicate', for the implication is that he wouldn't go to bed with anyone as old as Lady Wishfort.

amour i.e. love affair.

Mrs Marwood 'Mrs' (an abbreviation of 'Mistress', e.g. 'Mistress Marwood') was generally used of all women, not just

28 The Way of the World

those who were married. Mirabell says that Mrs Marwood gave the game away to Lady Wishfort.
omissions of that nature i.e. failures (to make love to them).
her prejudice i.e. her bias (in favour of).
confesses you are conscious ... the lady Fainall and Mirabell are sparring, with Mirabell aware of Fainall's interest in Mrs Marwood, and Fainall trying to discover whether Mirabell has, in the past, made love to Mrs Marwood, and then slighted her.
the last canonical hour i.e. that period of the morning (from 8 a.m. to noon) when marriages could take place.
jade Originally the reference was to an inferior or overworked horse, but it is also a term of contempt for a woman.

(Act 1, Scene 2)

the grand affair High-flown language to describe the marriage of Waitwell and Foible.
something tedious i.e. a long time.
coupling at Pancras i.e. marriage at St Pancras Church.
as 'twere in a country dance Although the simile comes from the servant we should make a note of it – for in a certain sense this kind of comedy *is* a dance, with a ritual of changing partners.
dispatch i.e. action.
Duke's Place St James's Church, Aldgate, where marriages could be performed quickly – and often illegally.
riveted in a trice Joined together (married) in a short time.
liveries i.e. distinctive clothes worn (here) by the servants.
shake his ears i.e. move quickly, get a move on.
Dame Partlet Foible, whom Waitwell has married. The reference is to Chaucer's *Nun's Priest's Tale* and to the hen, Dame Pertelote.
Rosamond's Pond Apparently where lovers met in St James's Park, a pond which was filled in in the latter part of the 18th century.
tender your ears i.e. as you value (the safety of) your ears.

(Act 1, Scene 3)

Cabal-night See note p.27. Here Mirabell refers to it because of the fear of discovery.
consequence i.e. of necessity.
suffer your wife i.e. allow her.
jealous i.e. suspicious (of her motives in going).
who are engaged i.e. who meet there, who attend.

too contemptible Fainall's ironic way of referring to Witwoud and Petulant.
who is not ... who is one Note the wit and the antithesis here.
her understanding i.e. her ability to choose her company
complaisance Politeness, deference (but there is irony in the remark).
I like her with all her faults Note this, for the understanding that Millamant and Mirabell reach later is based on mutual knowledge of each other; the real knowledge, not the romantic illusion.
so natural ... artful i.e. natural to her, or cunningly put on.
used me Tested me.
sifted weighed.
by rote I learned them by heart.
as familiar to me as my own frailties i.e. her faults are as well known to me as my own.
I shall like 'em as well This is a fine insight into human nature and more particularly our capacity for self-love, wrily recognized here by Mirabell.
you are your own man again i.e. you will really discover yourself (in your happiness).
and so forth Fainall is perhaps, with these words, referring to additional, extramarital 'experience'.

(Act 1, Scene 4; Scene 5)

he is half-brother to this ... cousins too Read this carefully, as it explains some of the complexity of the plot.
I had rather be his relation A direct acknowledgement of his wish to marry Millamant.
is above i.e. more than.
honour of England ... blockheads of all ages An example of Fainall's 'wit'.
prohibit the exportation of fools Mirabell is mocking excessive law-making – another example of his 'wit'.
trade with a little loss ... overstocked Note the commercial imagery – but the implication is that fools are better exported than 'overstocking' the country.
knight-errant ... anything related Heavy irony – 'this chivalrous man ... is he anything like his brother?'
like a medlar grafted on a crab Nature imagery it may be, but it is singularly tart wit – a medlar is a kind of bitter wild plum, and crab-apples have a very sour taste. Medlars are eaten when decayed, hence the reference to 'pulp' as Fainall follows through with the image.

when he's drunk, he's as loving as the monster in 'The Tempest' Stephano and Trinculo get Caliban drunk (see *The Tempest*, Act 2, Scene 2).
commonplace of comparisons This is Witwoud's notebook, containing similes that he will use later to demonstrate his 'wit'.
not exceptious He does not take offence (take exception to ...).
the reputation of understanding raillery He likes everyone to think that he understands the nature of the ridicule being practised.

(Act 1, Scene 6)

afford i.e. grant.
as heavy as a panegyric ... commendatory verses Obviously comparisons from his 'book', but satirical about the extreme expressions to which death on the one hand and flattery on the other give rise.
epistle dedicatory i.e. the preface to the poets patron at the beginning of the play. One would like to think that through Witwoud Congreve is mocking a practice which he himself employed – but we cannot be sure.
but half a fool Mirabell is of course implying that Witwoud is a complete one.
le Drole i.e. the witty man.
at once so foreign and domestic The coinage is not original, for these were the headings under which the news was set out in the papers of the time. Witwoud is using the convention that it was common *not* to be close to one's wife (hence 'foreign') except in name (hence 'domestic').
like an old maid at a marriage ... My dear Witwoud, one suspects, affects a rather effeminate tone throughout.
I thank you heartily Notice the speed of Mirabell's repartee.
spleen Bad temper.
breed debates i.e. initiate arguments.
a very pretty fellow Attractive, but without dignity.
troth Truly, upon my word.
if he had any judgement in the world Notice how Witwoud quite deliberately reverses what he has said he would do – he 'wrongs' Petulant and then blames Fainall ('don't detract from the merits of my friend').
over-nicely bred i.e. of good breeding, refined; this can be glossed as 'he is not over-particular' – as we would say today, 'I'm not too happy about it', 'not too sure'.
bum-bailey The bailiff sent to extract money for debt.
fire and life A term which Witwoud is careful not to define, in case it may reflect credit on his friend!

Act summaries, critical commentary, textual notes and revision questions 31

unsincere Note the valuation of insincerity as 'a trifle' — a pointer to the low moral level of a society that thinks thus.
a wit should no more be sincere, than a woman constant This 'wit' defines the morality of the times, with its emphasis on the superficial. But we should not equate Congreve's views with those of his creatures — in fact this kind of exposure is itself a condemnation of such standards.
a decay of parts i.e. a deterioration of the mind or the intellect.
positive i.e. self-opinionated.
natural parts i.e. how simple he is (a 'natural' is something of an idiot).
wants i.e. lacks.
unseasonable i.e. unwelcome.
wit ... evasion i.e. he has not the intelligence to conceal.
porter i.e. doorkeeper.

(Act 1, Scene 7)

brave Petulant i.e. bold, noble.
dishes i.e. cups.
cinnamon-water Powdered cinnamon with hot water, sugar and spirit, supposed to help the digestion.

(Act 1, Scene 8)

That i.e. the cinnamon-water.
strumpets Prostitutes.
bawd One who procures prostitutes.
trulls Prostitutes.
coach-hire, and something more by the week He pays for their travelling in the coach and gives them something over an above that.
before he found out this way Before he thought of this device to draw attention to himself.
slip you out i.e. leave surreptitiously.
whip ... trip ... clap ... slap Note the rhyming — almost a mockery of the full-rhymed verse of tragedy — and the onomatopoeic effect of speed thus conveyed.
sometimes leave a letter for himself The whole passage underlines the premium placed on *appearances* in life as distinct from its reality. Though this is very humorous, there is also something pathetic in the loneliness and the need to be noticed that can drive one to this kind of deception.

32 The Way of the World

(Act 1, Scene 9)

stays i.e. waits.
'Sbud 'God's blood' (swearing).
professed midwife ... professed whoremaster The services of both are liable to be needed at any time; though the difference indicates authorial irony at Petulant's lack of distinction between them.
Pox on 'em Curse them.
All's one i.e. it's all the same to me.
persons of condition i.e. fashionable ladies of high rank.
a dried fig i.e. worth nothing.
or rub off, if I want appetite or clear off, leave, if I have no inclination for them.
sultana queens ... Roxolanas. Roxolana (a sultana = sultan's wife) appears in D'Avenant's play *The Siege of Rhodes*, the first part of which was produced in 1656.
Cry you mercy A mocking way of saying 'I beg your pardon.'
Harkee i.e. listen (you).
caterwauling The noise made by cats on heat, hence derogatory of the 'old aunt'.
conventicle A meeting (often clandestine) of Nonconformists.
come off i.e. get away with it, explain it away.
trundle i.e. leave.
Anger helps complexion i.e. it will give them a good colour and save cosmetics.
continence ... dissembled i.e. this self-control is all lies.
your interpreter i.e. he will ask Witwoud what he (Petulant) means.
All's one for that It is of no consequence, it doesn't matter. (See previous note.)
snug's the word, I shrug Keep quiet, bound to secrecy, I don't want to get involved.
raillery Mockery.
thy competitor in fame i.e. your equal in reputation.
a dead whiting's eye by a pearl of orient Note that this is an example of Mirabell's rather more outspoken and direct 'wit'.
than Mercury is by the sun Mercury is the planet nearest the sun, but owing to its eccentric orbit it is visible for only about two hours before or after sunset.
wo't i.e. will.
Pshaw An expression indicative of contempt.
an uncertain woman i.e. unpredictable.
I thought you had died for her i.e. that you would be prepared to die for her.
demme The affectation of 'Damn me'.

Act summaries, critical commentary, textual notes and revision questions 33

Cleopatra The legendary Egyptian Queen (69–60 BC) who enslaved, among others, Mark Antony.
at some distance i.e. reserved towards one another.
worse than a Quaker hates a parrot i.e. because the parrot repeats the swearing it overhears and thus offends the ears of anyone belonging to a strict religious sect.
a fishmonger hates a hard frost i.e. it is then difficult to get at the fish.
items of such a treaty being in embryo i.e. indications that such an idea had already been thought of (the uncle marrying Millamant).
fobbed i'faith Truly cheated (of having Millamant).
humourist i.e. she is whimsical.
The quintessence Of the major importance. Petulant is being both pedantic and self-conceited.
they never mind him i.e. never pay any attention to him.
tête à tête i.e. yes, intimately, in intimate moments.
soft i.e. easy-going or easily kept quiet.
silly i.e. without much grasp of the situation.
the Mall Fashionable walk by St James's Park.
we'll be very severe i.e. in our remarks upon others.
putting the ladies out of countenance i.e. upsetting them (by your conversation).
their innocence by not understanding Petulant displays a knowledge of human nature here – either they don't understand our suggestive remarks, or they should have the discretion to pretend not to.
Where modesty's ill manners Note the concluding couplet, which is not merely a Restoration convention, but was used as far back as the Elizabethan period, by Shakespeare.

Revision questions on Act 1

1 Outline the plot so far in *The Way of the World*.
2 What do you learn of Mirabell and Fainall in this act?
3 Compare and contrast Witwoud and Petulant as they appear so far.
4 Write a short appreciation of the nature of the comedy in this act.

Act 2

Mrs Fainall and Mrs Marwood (note the irony, since at this stage Mrs Fainall does not know that Mrs Marwood is her husband's mistress) discuss men and love, Mrs Marwood revealing that her own supposed aversion to men is a mask in order to allow herself more freedom with them. But when she extracts from Mrs Fainall the admission that she hates her husband, Mrs Marwood says that she has merely been testing her. As the conversation proceeds it becomes obvious that Mrs Marwood is attracted to Mirabell – who then enters with Fainall. Mrs Fainall goes off with Mirabell, and Mrs Marwood with Fainall. The latter accuses Mrs Marwood of loving Mirabell, and takes her to task for ruining Mirabell's relationship with Millamant by disclosing his previous false advances to Lady Wishfort. They quarrel vehemently, and Fainall's mercenary motives in marrying his wife come to light. He now seeks even more from her. Fainall soothes Mrs Marwood; and the pair are now replaced on the scene by Mrs Fainall and Mirabell. It is revealed that it was Mirabell who persuaded her to marry Fainall, and Mirabell now confides to her his plot about his 'pretended uncle'. When this 'uncle' has become contracted to Lady Wishfort, Mirabell will expose the 'imposture' and, by saving the lady, gain her consent for his marriage to Millamant.

At this stage Millamant enters. She displays a striking 'wit' herself, the sequence on her 'pinning up her hair' (to curl it) with letters being particularly brilliant; she uses only those written in verse! There are some fine verbal passages here similar to those exchanged by Beatrice and Benedict in *Much Ado About Nothing*. Millamant says that she will not have Mirabell, but reveals that she knows of his plot. Alone Mirabell speaks of his love; and Foible and Waitwell, earthily reflecting their own pleasures, report on the shaping of the plot. Waitwell is now to be 'Sir Rowland'.

We move from male conversation and intrigue to women's conversation and intrigue: Congreve deliberately uses ironic contrast to point up the particular aspects of plot development. His sense of structure is also apparent. Affectation is a key issue in the play – one is inclined to say that it is a way of life – and we see this in Mrs Fainall's affected hatred of men. There is a strong emphasis – with sexual innuendo – on the sufferings of women in love (and in life) – but at the same time an insistence on living (and loving) freely for the moment: her pretence of hatred is thus exposed. Mrs Marwood further compliments Mrs Fainall by saying that she can only be frank with a friend: again the indications of hypocrisy are apparent, for she is really intent on concealing both motives and relationships. The 'game' is being played in this dialogue between the two women, which reveals the areas of appearance and reality. Blushing and pallor are used as markers for the real nature of feeling. Fainall shows how clever and cunning he has been (and how jealous, though he has of course concealed it), but the row he has with Mrs Marwood brings real feelings to the surface as distinct from simulated ones. The dramatic temperature is raised, but the game of concealment has to be resumed with the entrance of Mirabell and, Mrs Fainall, their balanced and sophisticated exchanges reflecting their outward lives. Interestingly Mrs Fainall, once Mirabell's mistress, now becomes his confidante, since she knows all about the plot and Mirabell's ultimate designs. At the same time, the vulnerability of women is being indicated. Note the immediate impact of Millamant, fittingly complementing Mirabell in terms of wit and repartee and, one suspects beneath this, in terms of feeling. Mincing's language is caricature refinement, further evidence of Congreve's excellent ear for affectations across the social spectrum. Millamant's superb speech beginning 'Why, one makes lovers ...' shows the pace of her wit and her own recognition of the affectation of 'love'. The wit flashes in her conversation with Mirabell, but we are aware of some strength of feeling between them: when she leaves with Mincing, Mirabell certainly reveals his own feelings for her. Waitwell and Foible contribute to the money and love themes on which the plot rests, Waitwell providing an instance of male complacency with regard to what he feels is his astute conditioning of Foible.

(Act 2, Scene 1)

in extremes i.e. of mood.
doting or averse i.e making a great fuss (of us) or being distant or cold.
jealousies are insupportable Their suspicions are unbearable.
ever die before us i.e. in front of our eyes (with the implication 'before we die too').

'tis better to be left, than never to have been loved Almost the equivalent of ' 'Tis better to have loved and lost/Than never to have loved at all' (Tennyson, *In Memoriam*, 1850).
the sweets of life i.e. the joys of loving.
wear and waste ... rust i.e. it will be used and not abused. The theme is, 'I will live for the present.'
you dissemble an aversion i.e. you pretend a hatred.
To be free To be open or frank (about it).
no taste of those insipid dry discourses i.e. I don't appreciate those dull conversations women have among themselves.
Love will resume ... lawful tyrant We shall fall in love again and be ruled by that passion.
You profess a libertine i.e. you speak like a woman of loose morals.
freedom Frankness.
transcendently Above all others.
meritoriously Deservedly.
vipers A common term of denigration and contempt at the time.
an Amazon a Penthesilea The latter was Queen of the Amazons, who were a famous race of warlike women. In the siege of Troy by the Greeks she came to the assistance of the Trojan King Priam, but was killed by Achilles.
by marrying i.e. in order to gain revenge. An example of Mrs Marwood's 'wit'.
sensible of ill-usage Aware of being badly treated.
cuckold The husband of an unfaithful wife.
I'd make him believe I did Here is the refinement, the subtlety of wit, and a further underlining of the appearance/reality *motif* throughout the play.
Why had not you as good do it Why don't you commit adultery anyway?
it dissembled i.e. that it was a lie.
a little sick o' the sudden i.e. I feel a little faint.
He turned short He looked upon me suddenly.
overcome me Taken me by surprise.

(Act 2, Scene 2)

My dear ... My soul Note the spontaneous hypocrisy of husband and wife.
He is the only man that does Implying, of course, that Mirabell thinks that she looks beautiful – he is indeed a true gallant.
what is an effect of my concern i.e. which shows how much I care for you.

a pleasant relation i.e. something interesting (you were telling us).
a humour i.e. a mood.
by being seen to walk with his wife Notice that this is the reverse of morality and reflects the fashion of the times. It is also part of the anti-marriage comment. (This reversal of accepted values was later to play a large part in the wit of Oscar Wilde, 1854–1900.)
I dare promise you will oblige us both i.e. you will please both my husband and me if you work with me.

(Act 2, Scene 3)

Ay! Yes! (But it is a loaded comment by Mrs Marwood, since she is Fainall's mistress.)
weep like Alexander A reference to Alexander the Great (356–324 BC), ruler of Macedonia, whose conquests extended to part of India.
tender of your honour i.e. concerned to preserve it.
insensible i.e. unfeeling, or even unaware.
I have seen the warm confession i.e. I have seen you blush.
'Twas for my ease to oversee i.e. for my own peace of mind I ignored (my wife's advances to Mirabell).
because the nodding husband ... the watchful lover slept Do you believe that because I pretended not to see what my wife was doing, I did not notice what you were getting up to yourself?
The injuries ... your interposing i.e. The wrongs (you have committed against him) ... your interference (the disclosure of Mirabell's false advances to Lady Wishfort).
easy nature i.e. gullible.
baseness i.e. lowness of nature.
unmindful of the merit i.e. ignoring the worthiness of what I have done.
meritorious ... vicious Note the antithesis – the meaning is that it should be to Mrs Marwood's credit with Fainall that she has maintained the deception of his wife.
slight account ... strictest ties i.e. your previous disparagement of the bonds that bind people together (marriage).
discovered i.e. (what you feel) is revealed.
own what has passed Mrs Marwood intends to act quickly if need be, and tell Mrs Fainall the truth about herself and Fainall.
Frenzy! Madness!
bankrupt in honour, as indigent of wealth The dual attack – on his honour and his poverty (were it not for his wife's fortune).

Your fame I have preserved i.e. your reputation has been safe with me.
prodigality Recklessly lavish.
moiety Half, in the legal sense.
Death Here, a curse ('God's death', usually rendered at that time as "sdeath'.)
a heart of proof i.e that can withstand anything (including the death his wife wishes for him).
the ways of wedlock and this world This anticipates Fainall's later cynical statement which gives the play its title.
asperse Like 'cast aspersions upon', accuse me falsely.
I'd leave 'em to get loose One of the few instances of *physical* violence as a result of emotional suffering in the play.
this is extravagance i.e. this is going too far.
easy in my doubts i.e. have peace of mind while I doubted you.
'Sdeath See note above.
You have a mask Commonly worn by women of fashion at the time, since it disguised them, protected them against discovery – another underlining of the appearance/reality theme.

(Act 2, Scene 4)

with prudence i.e. moderation. Mirabell can be eminently reasonable.
I have loved with indiscretion A double meaning, referring to her past love for Mirabell and her marrying her husband.
To save that idol reputation One of the key phrases of the play, since honour, reputation, appearance in the eyes of the fashionable world is what matters to its inhabitants.
lavish i.e. loose-living.
interested and professing Interested in himself and pretending to be my friend.
that woman stand excused i.e. make her blameless in reputation.
A better ... a worse Again note the antithetical balance of the phrase, much like the balance of an heroic couplet.
made you privy Secretly confided in you.
your pretended uncle i.e. the person who will impersonate your uncle.
your interest i.e. your service, your way of looking at things.
and worn i.e. married (and bedded).
like Mosca in 'The Fox' A reference back to a 'humours' comedy by Ben Jonson (1573–1637), *Volpone, or The Fox* – in which Mosca preys on his master, learns all his secrets, and threatens to reveal them unless he is given half his master's fortune.

sure i.e. safe.
caught in a contract i.e. trapped into a marriage.
discover the imposture betimes Reveal the trick to her in good time.
a certificate of her gallant's former marriage i.e. of Waitwell's ('Sir Rowland's') marriage to Foible.
seem to carry it more privately Carry out the affair more secretly.
I have an opinion i.e. I am optimistic.
what a butler could pinch out of a napkin The image indicates that servants can share the affectations of people of fashion – setting out a napkin to best advantage by pinching it into an attractive shape.
feel the craving of a false appetite i.e. sexual desire.
'Tis the green-sickness of a second-childhood i.e. adolescent yearnings in old age.

(Act 2, Scene 5)

fan spread ... streamers out This kind of image is used elsewhere, notably by Milton in *Samson Agonistes*, and in Dryden's *An Evening's Love* (1668).
A shoal of fools for tenders i.e small ships attending a large one; but Mirabell is exaggerating.
sculler i.e. a small boat rowed by two sculls, pulled by one man.
Beau-monde Fashionable society.
perukes Wigs (worn at the time by all men of fashion).
As a favourite just disgraced The reference is obviously political, and this is equally obviously another gleaning from Witwoud's commonplace-book.
truce with your similitudes i.e. let's agree not to have any more of your (trite) comparisons.
As a physician of a good air But Witwoud is sharp – bad 'air' causes diseases, and keeps a doctor in work.
I do blaze i.e. I am in good form.
asked ... a new fashion Millamant is declaring here (deliberately in modishly trivial terms) that she has been enquiring after Mrs Fainall as diligently as she would seek news of a new fashion, probably in dress.
truce with your similitudes Witwoud is demonstrating his 'wit' by employing the phrase sharply in return.
enquiring after an old fashion i.e. something that is out of date, to expect to see a husband and wife concerned about one another.

40 The Way of the World

'a hit, a hit, a palpable hit' An echo of *Hamlet*, Act 5, Scene 2, where Osric records Hamlet's first successful sword thrust at Laertes.
abroad i.e. out.
mem Madam.
laship Ladyship.
They serve one to pin up one's hair Evidence of Millamant's superb independence, her own satirical shaft at those who are always rushing their emotions into print, a marvellous piece of affectation too. (See also the section on *Style*.)
I find I must keep copies Witwoud, rather ponderously, joins in the game; as a 'wit' he mustn't be left behind in this affectation.
Only with those in verse Millamant is, however, too much for him.
tift and tift i.e. arranged, titivated, worked at her hair.
crips Crisp; the pronunciation underlines Mincing's own 'refined' accents, which are always ludicrous because of their exaggerated refinement.
such a critic Even this exchange carries its own irony; Witwoud is not a critic, and Mincing wouldn't know one if she saw one.
exceptions i.e. offence.
your true vanity is in the power of pleasing i.e. you really like yourself best when you have given pleasure.
beauty is the lover's gift This fine paragraph carries the belief that a person who is loved becomes beautiful – through their lover's admiration and praise.
Fainall i.e. Mrs Fainall.
if one pleases one makes more i.e. we 'affect' love whenever our imagination or 'humour' wants us to.
card-matches Matches made of cardboard, their tips dipped in sulphur.
want a being i.e. lack a presence.
lover ... echo A fine antithesis.
Draw off i.e. leave us.

(Act 2, Scene 6)

physic Medicine.
assafoetida This is a resin with an unpleasantly strong smell of garlic; used medicinally. (Usually spelt with one 's'.)
not to have you i.e. in marriage or sexually – Millamant has the verve and personality to mean both.
distemper Ailment.
I think But this in fact shows her uncertainty.
as win a woman with plain-dealing and sincerity But this

statement shows the sincerity of Mirabell's love and provides a
moral underpinning to the superficiality which constitutes the
action of the play.
Like Solomon at the dividing of the child It was quite
common for scenes from the Old Testament to be worked into
tapestries. The reference here is to 1 Kings, 3,16–28.
merry i e. jocular, flippant.
a watchlight i.e. a nightlight or long-burning candle.
Without the help of the devil This paragraph shows Millamant
in complete control, for she has just revealed that she knows of
Mirabell's plot. But the secret of how she found out is hers.

(Act 2, Scene 7)

mind and mansion i.e. peace of mind and of living.
windmill ... whimsical ... woman Congreve often uses poetic
devices in his prose, and here the alliteration conveys the
movement of Mirabell's mind.
to which they cannot turn i.e. women, and their whims.
motion not method is their occupation i.e. fickleness – 'they
let their hearts rule their heads' is the burden of Mirabell's
thought.
reason ... instinct Notice that instinct (love) wins: sufficient
proof of Mirabell's – and Congreve's – sincerity of purpose.
pair of turtles i.e. lovers.
Valentine's Day 14th February, a martyr's day, but associated
with love and the sending of a card to the beloved. Here
Mirabell obviously means the term to comment ironically on his
own love-match for Waitwell and Foible.

(Act 2, Scene 8)

recreation Pleasure.
solacing in lawful delights i.e. making love (lawful because
they are married).
directions ... instructions Waitwell's remarks contain obvious
sexual innuendo.
Give you joy I greet you happily.
inquietudes i.e. worrying (about her).
That I believe Droll understatement on Mirabell's part.
I think she has profited Waitwell's sexual innuendo – and
satisfaction – continues.
Spouse Waitwell is implying that now she is married Foible
should hand over the money to him.
lease ... farm Obviously already promised by Mirabell to them
if the plan succeeds.

at her toilet In the process of dressing.
and prevent her i.e. get there before her.
B'w'y God be with you.

(Act 2, Scene 9)

pert ... preferment Forward, saucy (because of) her new (married) status.
transform i.e. change yourself.
attended i.e. waited upon (in his new status of 'Sir Rowland').
acquaintance ... familiarity i.e. get to know myself again.
To lose my title... i.e. cease being 'Sir Rowland', but find I am still married.

Revision questions on Act 2

1 Give an account of the part played by Mrs Marwood in this act.

2 What evidence is there that the author is taking a moral stance himself in this act?

3 Write an essay on the quality of the humour in this act.

Act 3

Lady Wishfort is waiting for news, brooding on her appearance and living on her nerves, when Mrs Marwood comes to see her. She has just seen Foible 'in conference with Mirabell'. At Lady Wishfort's suggestion, Mrs Marwood retires to the closet so that her hostess may more freely interrogate her maid Foible when she arrives. Foible 'gets away' with it. She emphasizes how 'taken' Sir Rowland is with the picture of Lady Wishfort; she prevails upon her to get ready and make herself as attractive as possible for Sir Rowland, this being the surest way of revenging herself upon Mirabell. (Meanwhile Mrs Marwood finds Lady Wishfort's closet an ideal listening-post!)

In the next sequence Mrs Fainall divulges to Foible her fears concerning Mrs Marwood; the plot is given away by them to the concealed and listening Mrs Marwood. Later, Mrs Marwood tells Lady Wishfort that Sir Wilfull and Millamant would make a good match, then further elaborates upon

Act summaries, critical commentary, textual notes and revision questions 43

her own plot by telling Millamant that the town knows all about her and Mirabell. After an argument, Petulant and Witwoud settle their quarrel; shortly afterwards. Sir Wilfull arrives, with his half-brother doing his best to ignore him. Eventually Sir Wilfull recognizes his brother – and indeed recognizes him for what he is. Fainall and Mrs Marwood converse apart, and Mrs Marwood urges Fainall to inform Lady Wishfort of her daughter's past affair with Mirabell. This will further malign Mirabell; Fainall will have his revenge for Mirabell's affair with his wife; and Mrs Marwood will send a letter to Lady Wishfort exposing Sir Rowland, thus further undermining Mirabell. The anti-marriage theme is very prominent at the end of this act.

Lady Wishfort controls the purse-strings, and is therefore at the centre of the play: Mrs Marwood now assumes an important function in the plot. There is pathos beneath the ridiculous loneliness of Lady Wishfort, and not a little farce in Peg misunderstanding what she wants. Of course she does need the drink, but in rather larger quantities than she gets it here. Notice the panic into which Lady Wishfort is thrown by Marwood's observation of Foible in conference with Mirabell – of course she does not know the true situation. The reference to the books shows the cover of respectability in this scene – and doubtless other scenes – of intrigue. Note the dramatic effectiveness – and dramatic irony – of the concealment of Marwood. Foible reveals that she was not in need of any conditioning by Waitwell – she relies on her own ingenuity to get her out of being suspected by Lady Wishfort. And she is adept at flattery, while her putting down of Mirabell to Lady Wishort only encourages the latter to express a passionate hatred which is a thin disguise for passionate love. But Foible, intent on Mirabell's plot, is achieving just what she wants – the unthinking commitment of Lady Wishfort to Sir Rowland. Yet Foible speaks truthfully when she says 'There are some cracks discernible in the white varnish', while the 'wall' comparison shows the separation between nature and appearance, the latter crumbling. The picture equals the mask which must be worn in society. Lady Wishfort's sexual appetite is clearly indicated in the language she employs to Foible about Sir Rowland, but as always she is intent on keeping up the appearance of her rank. The dramatic temperature rises with the entrance of Mrs Fainall, her words directly referring to the concealed 'devil' Marwood: she gives away the plot directly and explicitly. The dialogue between Foible and Mrs Fainall, with every word a piece of invaluable information to the listening Marwood, shows Congreve's craftsmanship. Marwood's soliloquy is also effective, and she is quick to work her will upon Lady Wishfort. The exchanges between Millamant and Marwood are laced with spiteful innuendo (remember Marwood is plotting for Millamant to marry Sir Wilfull). Millamant has some wonderfully catty lines. Witwoud and Petulant perform their now usual double act — both at the mercy of shafts from Millamant and Marwood — before the entrance of Sir Wilfull. Immediately the town–country contrast is stressed. Sir Wilfull's exchange with the servant shows how quick-changing city life is — and the servant's failure to identify one 'gallant' from another is a moral comment on the promiscuity of that life. The falseness, indeed baseness, of city life is further emphasized in the Petulant/Witwoud 'smoking' of Sir Wilfull, who takes the opportunity (after his own affectionate greeting) to respond to Witwoud's ''tis not modish to know relations in town' with 'the fashion's a fool; and you're a fop, dear brother'. There follows a devastating exposure of the fop by the country brother. In fact Witwoud is stripped of his mask, and before Petulant too! Sir Wilfull continues to let himself and his company down, and we find ourselves warming to him because of this. Mrs Marwood successfully stirs it up with Fainall, inciting him to revenge against Mirabell. This is the shallow way of the world. Fainall's bitterness is traceable to the double theme of loss of money and, as he thinks, being cuckolded. Notice the economic way (in both senses of the word) in which Marwood produces her plot to Fainall. The imagery of war is appropriately used to underline the excessive extent of Marwood's ideas. But they need to be excessive to convince Fainall that she doesn't covet Mirabell herself.

(Act 3, Scene 1)

veracity Truth.
the red i.e. rouge, paint, makeup.

Act summaries, critical commentary, textual notes and revision questions 45

arrant Absolute, real. (The word is usually employed in a derogatory sense, as in 'arrant knave' = 'an out-and-out rogue'.)
Mopus Person noted for dullness, stupidity.
the Spanish paper Rouge on paper imported from Spain.
changeling Child substituted for another by stealth, especially elf child left by fairies.
like bobbins Reels of thread.
come at i.e. find immediately.
fetch me the cherry-brandy i.e. a drink will put colour in her cheeks – and console her.

(Act 3, Scene 2)

Mrs Qualmsick Probably always worried, rundown and ill because she is eternally pregnant.
Save thee God bless you!

(Act 3, Scene 3)

fairy ... acorn Obviously the cup is very small.
brass thimble ... nutmeg These were charms meant to bring good luck; here Lady Wishfort is obviously continuing her sarcasm regarding the small cup Peg has brought.
like a tapster Person employed to serve drinks.
Maritornes the Asturian The chambermaid in *Don Quixote*, Cervantes's famous novel (first part published in 1605, second part, 1615).

(Act 3, Scene 4)

in *dishabillé* Only partly dressed, a careless toilet; a corruption of the French *en déshabille* or *déshabillé(e)*.
a lost thing Little does she know the truth. Foible is indeed 'lost' in a different sense – lost to Lady Wishfort's confidence.
I'm undone i.e. ruined.
freedom Frankness.
Quarles and Prynne, and the 'Short View of the Stage' No one can accuse Lady Wishfort of being anything but proper in her reading. (Francis Quarles (1592–1644) was a religious poet, William Prynne (1600–69), the author of an attack upon the stage before the closing of the playhouses by the Puritans; Jeremy Collier (1650–1726) had written *A Short View of the Immorality and Profaneness of the English Stage* (1698) to which Congreve had written a somewhat ineffectual reply.)
Bunyan's works John Bunyan (1628–88) the great dissenting author of *The Pilgrim's Progress* and some sixty other works.

(Act 3, Scene 5)

the party i.e. Sir Rowland.
The miniature i.e. the picture of herself.
counted like A good resemblance.
detected me i.e. given me away.
had a fling i.e. made fun of.
I could not hold i.e. I could no longer keep silent.
I gave him his own i.e. I answered him strongly.
fleers Sneers, mockery.
catering ... ferreting Assisting ... nosing about.
disbanded i.e. no longer employed.
half pay i.e. the officer's pension.
come down pretty deep i.e. pay up generously.
superannuated Too old for anything, hence discarded.
Ods God's.
I'll have him i.e. I'll see that he pays for this.
a drawer i.e. one who draws intoxicating drinks.
Robin from Lockets A writer from a restaurant in Charing Cross.
I'll fit you i.e. stop you.
frippery Cast-off clothes (meaning Lady Wishfort).
I'll handle you i.e. deal with you (but there is a sexual note as well).
Incontinently i.e. at once.
a tatterdemallion One dressed in rags and tatters (nowadays spelt with one 'l').
Long-Lane penthouse Long Lane held a number of second-hand clothes shops (Lady Wishfort is extending the 'frippery' idea) and this refers to the shed where they would be stored.
gibbet-thief A thief hanged on the gallows.
as the million lottery Government-sponsored lottery to raise one million pounds.
the whole court upon a birthday A comment on the extravagance which required courtiers to wear expensive clothes on the King's birthday.
Ludgate The prison used for debtors. It was in Blackfriars.
angle ... for brass farthings Begging through the grate of the prison by hanging out a glove for the money.
any economy She has ruined her make-up, which cost money, and it will cost more to put it right.
arrantly flayed i.e. her skin is thoroughly lined and peeling. (See note p.45.)
keep up to my picture i.e. I shan't live up to what he expects (having seen the miniature of me).
a little art i.e. on the painter's account.

Act summaries, critical commentary, textual notes and revision questions 47

Your picture must sit for you i.e. we must make you up like it.
will a' Will he.
come ... importunate ... push All indicate Lady Wishfort's obsession with sex, for all suggest sexual advances.
break decorums i.e. let myself down, I'll behave properly.
if I am forced to advance i.e. make the first approaches (she means amorous ones) to him.
breaking her forms Abandoning her customary standards.
A little scorn Foible repeats these words of Lady Wishfort's, and injects her own irony into them.
My niece affects it ... wants features Lady Wishfort is saying that Millamant tries to get this effect . . but she lacks the good looks.
importunes i.e. begs me (to grant him favours).

(Act 3, Scene 6)

Discover i.e. reveal.
personate i.e. impersonate.
the former good correspondence i.e. when Mrs Fainall was Mirabell's mistress.
I worked her up ... as they say of a Welsh maidenhead I have so excited her ... that she will yield to him easily and completely.
a month's mind i.e. a strong liking for (Mirabell).

(Act 3, Scene 7)

Mrs Engine i.e. Foible, who has set the plot going.
passe-partout Mrs Marwood, in her next words, correctly translates this as a 'master-key'.
it's over with you i.e. the affair she (Mrs Fainall) had with Mirabell.
to procure for him i.e. to help Mirabell get Millamant.
The devil's an ass Presumably from Jonson's play of that name in 1631.
a driveller i.e. talking foolishly.
horns i.e. which signify the cuckold, the betrayed husband.
panting ripe i.e. with love (and lust) at the thought of Sir Rowland.
like any chymist on the day of projection i.e. the alchemist's calculation that this is just the time to turn base metal into gold.

(Act 3, Scene 8)

an olio of affairs This is perhaps Lady Wishfort's rendering of 'an imbroglio' = a complicated situation.

(Act 3, Scene 10)

into a flame Expression of temper.
fit Fought. (Mincing's word for the past tense of 'fight'. We can still hear the word when the old American Negro spiritual 'Joshua Fit the Battle of Jericho' is sung.)
doily-stuff Light woollen cloth.
drap-de-berry From the province of Berry in France – another woollen cloth.
Mrs Primley's Note the ironic choice of name.
it burnishes Grows polished (pregnant).
no more conceal it i.e. your love.
Rhenish-wine tea The wine taken to reduce fatness.
a discarded toast i.e. one whose health was once drunk, but is now no longer in favour.

(Act 3, Scene 11)

nettled Angry.
mitigate those violent airs i.e. cease those angry movements.
complaisance i.e. deference.
so particular ... so insensible So attentive to Millamant and so unmoved by everything else.
a little barbarous somewhat cruel.
I did not mind you I did not take any account of you.
a sybil Prophetess, sorceress.
and within a year or two as young Millamant cannot resist being catty about Mrs Marwood.
If you could but stay i.e. if you could remain the same age.
Your merry note Mrs Marwood is of course referring to her own suggestion (unknown to Millamant) that Millamant should marry Sir Wilfull.

(Act 3, Scene 12)

to comb i.e. their wigs.
agreeable to my honour It suits my mood.
SONG, I, II, III
Love's but i.e. 'Love must be ambitious' is the theme here, a direct comment on the action of the play.
pierc'd a swain ... inferior beauties sigh'd in vain i.e. Millamant has chosen the song, which reflects Mirabell's love for her. We can deduce that Mrs Marwood would be numbered among the 'inferior beauties'.
That heart which others bleed for, bleed for me i.e. the love of Mirabell, which she has.

(Act 3, Scene 13)

hit off a little wit i.e. spark off argument.
my cue i.e. when to rise (to contradiction).
two battledores i.e. the rackets used when hitting the shuttlecocks in the game of battledore and shuttlecock (which was the precursor of badminton).
positive ... presumptive Note the play on words, almost like a legal quibble.
very learnedly handled Mrs Marwood is being sarcastic about their pedantic humour.
on his parts i.e. natural wit. The implication is that he has very little. There is also a coarse play on 'sexual organs' for 'parts'.
The ordinary's paid for setting the Psalm The prison chaplain. (Jeffares includes an interesting note from Pope, who said that it was customary for those condemned to death at Tyburn to sing a Psalm.)
a man may do it without book i.e. die or make love without legal sanction.

(Act 3, Scene 14)

Bartlemew and his Fair Bartholomew's Fair was held annually at Smithfield on St Bartholomew's Day. Jonson wrote a play called *Bartholomew Fair*, first performed in 1614 but not published until 1631.
since the Revolution i.e. of 1688, when William and Mary replaced James II.
longer than anybody in the house An indictment of Lady Wishfort's moods and her treatment of those under her.
swear to her face in a morning, before she is dressed A comic reference to the fact that her makeup is elaborate afterwards.
gallants i.e. young men of fashion.

(Act 3, Scene 15)

Oons God's wounds. (A swear-word of the time; sometimes 'zounds'.)
knows less than a starling Sir Wilfull probably means that the starling, a clever mimic, cannot really know the meaning of the sounds it reproduces – anyone who 'knows less' must be ignorant indeed.
the Devil take him Curse him.
smoke him Take note of him, get ready to mock him.

thereafter ... meant It depends what you mean (by your remarks).
S'life God's life.
so I write myself i.e. sign myself.
'Sheart By God's heart; another contemporary swear-word.
the Wrekin A high hill in his home county, Shropshire.
becravated, and so beperriwigged i.e. so fashionably wearing a cravat and wig.
Odso by God.
a flap-dragon Valueless, worth no more than a small, dried edible fruit (from raisins put in the mouth after being taken from burning brandy and then extinguished).
hare's scut Its tail.
Inns o' Court breeding i.e. where lawyers are trained before practising.
not modish Not fashionable.
lubberly Clumsy, stupid.
slabber Slobber.
a call of Serjeants Serjeants-at-law are admitted to the bar, the implication here being one of celebration, all of them obtaining this advancement at the same time.
The fashion's a fool One wonders if this is spoken from the playwright's heart as well.
a subpoena A summons requiring the recipient to attend court.
Honoured Brother i.e. a ponderous, stiff and formal beginning to a letter.
Rat me Rot me.
a cock and a bull i.e. a fantastic story, not to be believed.
Pumple-Nose i.e. one with a pimple.
Furnival's Inn Attached to Lincoln's Inn.
Gazettes News-sheets.
Dawks's Letter Weekly paper.
Weekly Bill A death sheet, of those who died in and near London.
to that man i.e. Sir Wilfull.
bound prentice i.e. as an apprentice, which of course he would find degrading.
Belike Perhaps.
if my mind hold i.e. if I feel as I do now.
the weather cock your companion A direct insult, for he is a slave to the changes of fashion.
the peace holds A reference to the Treaty of Ryswick (1697) with France. It was later broken.
designed for France i.e. had determined to go to France.
at all adventures At all cost.
dainty Particular, choosy.

shill I, shall I i.e. being undecided (shilly-shallying).
a small matter A short time.
lingo i.e. your manner of speaking.
a spice A taste of, a touch of.
refined like a Dutch skipper i.e. totally *un*refined.

(Act 3, Scene 16)

a raillier One who indulges in mockery.
to choose As they wish, at their own choice.

(Act 3, Scene 17)

impatient i.e. it is ready, and has been for some time.
unbred Ill-mannered.

(Act 3, Scene 18)

rank-husband A corrupt, 'rotten' husband.
all in The Way of the World As things happen in this life, this society.
satyr A mythological creature, half-man, half-goat.
a citizen's child The child of one who is cuckolded.
out-stripped by my wife i.e. she has been even more unfaithful than he has.
scurvy wedlock i.e. contemptible marriage.
fond Foolish.
like a deputy-lieutenant's hall Apparently the hall was decorated with antlers.
given up her game i.e. stopped being Mirabell's mistress.
composition i.e. terms.
flag Falter.
this has an appearance This certainly promises well.
drink like a Dane The Danes were reputed to be heavy drinkers.
set his hand in See to it that he starts drinking.
who has not wherewithal to stake i.e. who can put up no guarantee.
cuckoldom ... honourable a root i.e. cuckoldom cannot discredit or dishonour anyone, since it springs from the honourable state of being married.
why not the branches? Mrs Marwood is continuing the association and is presumably referring to the cuckold's horns.
play the incendiary i.e. stir things up.
she knows some passages i.e. our own relationship.
let the mine be sprung i.e. the trap.
to grass Put her out, get rid of her.
partake Share.

will herd no more ... wear the badge ... disown the order Mixed images that underline Fainall's rejection of the married state.

All husbands must As with the endings of the previous acts, the anti-marriage theme is uppermost. (Remember that Congreve, despite his own liaisons, remained a bachelor.)

Revision questions on Act 3

1 Write an account of the effect produced by the arrival of Sir Wilfull Witwoud.

2 In what ways is Lady Wishfort grotesque? Refer closely to the text in your answer.

3 Indicate the part played by Mrs Marwood in this act.

4 What do you find humorous in the characters of Witwoud and Petulant?

Act 4

Lady Wishfort and Foible are together, the former preparing to receive 'Sir Rowland'. Millamant is still considering Mirabell, with Foible stressing his anxiety to see her. Then Sir Wilfull approaches Millamant, but without as yet the necessary drink to give him the courage to propose to her. Millamant persuades him to leave, and then entertains Mirabell. In exchanges of searing honesty, and with further indictment of what marriage can so often become, they yet agree to accept one another; the scene must be read very closely to gain the full impact of the wit and of the nature of the 'contract'.

Mrs Fainall arrives, urges Millamant to have Mirabell, then describes the disturbance Sir Wilfull is causing by his drunkenness. Petulant too, becomes drunk; and Millamant, having had quite enough, leaves Lady Wishfort with Sir Wilfull.

'Sir Rowland' is becoming impatient, and is eventually admitted to Lady Wishfort's presence; their scene together has a nice touch of slapstick. Foible manages to have a word with 'Sir Rowland' and Lady Wishfort calls in the dancers to entertain herself and 'Sir Rowland'. But following this, a letter is handed to Lady Wishfort describing 'Sir Rowland' as 'a cheat and a rascal'. Foible is sufficiently quick-witted to get 'Sir Rowland' to say that the letter was written by his nephew (Mirabell); then he departs to get a black box containing all his estate papers.

Lady Wishfort's preparations – and her appetite –make good visual as well as verbal comedy. There is a fine play on 'killing well', outwardly flattering but with a double meaning. There is some fine irony in the fact that Lady Wishfort is intent on posing – a deception calculated to attract 'Sir Rowland', who is himself a deception. The rhythms of her speech indicate her sensual pulse-rate. The scene between Millamant and Sir Wilfull has her quoting poetry to the accompaniment of his increasing tipsiness as he tries to get up the courage to propose – a farcical element is apparent. Again we get a deliberate contrast between town and country sounded in the text. Mirabell's continuation of the quotation of Waller's poem immediately establishes him as being in sympathy with Millamant and of course contrasts effectively with the verbal (and physical) blundering about of Sir Wilfull. The imagery and the wit in the exchanges between Millamant and Mirabell are very significant. Millamant shows an awareness of her own attractions. They balance each other perfectly in their expressed determination to have their own way – the verbal war of the sexes covering the feelings and their obvious sympathetic affinity. Congreve uses the occasion to mock loving matrimonial displays in public, as well as revealing more fully the individuality of Millamant. The latter's speeches ring with the independence from convention. The overwhelming effect conveyed is that marriage is acceptable only if each partner retains his/her individuality. Mirabell's ideas and innuendoes are more superficially and specifically sexual. The exchange amounts to a brilliant parody of what passes for marriage and the conventions and fashions and social responsibilities which attend it. The constant play on 'have' also carries the direct sexual innuendo. Mrs Fainall's news of Sir Wilfull's behaviour shows the contrasting chaos in the other part of the plot – here all is order – and Millamant's confession of her love for Mirabell is moving. The Witwoud–Petulant exchange provides another level of comedy, though even here the verbal play is apparent. Sir Wilfull in his cups becomes extremely crude. The attempts to remove Sir Witwoud are farcical. 'Sir Rowland's' entrance calls forth a spate of alliterative elegance from the impatient Lady Wishfort. The supposed reduction of Mirabell is grotesque, contributing to the slapstick nature of the comedy here. Perhaps Lady Wishfort's denial of her own sexual appetites is the high point of the farce, but with her exit and Waitwell's telling 'she is the antidote to desire' we come to appreciate the pace at which this act is moving – there is no let up in the visual dramatic tension. This reaches its climax with the reading of Marwood's letter exposing 'Sir Rowland', and is even enhanced by the speed with which Foible responds to the challenge. Lady Wishfort, perhaps too easily duped, is characteristically concerned for her reputation. Foible, who appears to have been successful, fittingly has the last word.

(Act 4, Scene 1)

sconces Wall-brackets to hold lights.
postilion One who rides the near horse of the leaders.
equipage i.e. the retinue.
pullvilled i.e. sprinkled with scented powder (to take away the smell).
with correspondence to his passion i.e. in harmony with his love.
Most killing well i.e. very attractive.
figure Attitude.
pretty disorder i.e. a little put out, attractively flustered-looking.
a levee i.e. arising, getting up.
furnishes Provides.
recomposing airs i.e. pulling myself together again.
set in to i.e. has begun.
Odds God's.

(Act 4, Scene 2)

There never yet was Woman made The beginning of a poem by Sir John Suckling (1609–42).
filthy verses i.e. licentious, ribald poems.
Thyrsis, A Youth of the Inspir'd Train The opening line of 'The Story of Phoebe and Daphne, Applied', a poem by Edmund Waller (1606–87).
philosophy to undergo a fool i.e. the balance to endure an idiot.
your proxy i.e. serve in place of you.

(Act 4, Scene 3)

pursue your point i.e. make your addresses.
wary Cautious.
break my mind i.e. tell her what I feel.
that I set on't i.e. I will go through with what I have begun.

(Act 4, Scene 4)

a'has i.e. she has.
a vixen trick i.e. a vicious, sharp trick.
I prithee spare me The first two lines of another poem by Suckling, which Millamant goes on to quote up to the end of its first verse.
Anan 'I beg your pardon?'
thy Power and Art The end of the verse – and ironic, if we consider the clumsiness of the approaches now being made.
Natural easy Suckling Praise for his flowing expression.
stripling i.e. youth. Sir Wilfull mistakes 'suckling' for a term of denigration.
Gothic i.e. rude or barbarian.
to fetch i.e. to take.
nauseate i.e. dislike intensely.
'tis like you may i.e. it's possible you do.
Ah l'étourdie Oh, the silly fool. (French, though the final 'e' should be omitted, since a *man* is being referred to.)
as time shall try i.e. as things fall out.
spare to speak and spare to speed i.e. if you don't say anything you won't achieve anything.
oblige me to leave me i.e. I shall be obliged if you will go.
all a case It's of no consequence.
it will keep cold i.e. it will still do, still be there.
Like Phoebus sang Another quotation from Waller's poem.
Phoebus and Daphne Apollo fell in love with her, pursued her and she was changed at her own request into a bay-tree, which became sacred to Apollo.

(Act 4, Scene 5)

Like Daphne she Mirabell continues the quotation.
curious i.e. difficult.
here the chase must end Mirabell is now cunningly referring to the legend which is the subject of the lines they have quoted – and of course applying it to his own case and that of Millamant.

I were wavering at the gate of a monastery Millamant's 'wit' — anyone less likely than she is to submit to a sudden conversion it would be hard to imagine.
the agreeable fatigues of solicitation i.e. the pleasant labours of being followed, having advances made to me.
independent of the bounty of his mistress i.e. apart from the gift (of her love) which his mistress confers upon him.
pragmatical Assured, complacent.
my will and pleasure i.e. having my own way, doing what I enjoy doing.
till after grace i.e. after the ceremony (of marriage).
douceurs, ye sommeils du matin i.e. pleasures (of the unmarried state), sleeping late into the morning.
I'll get up Mirabell has the spirit of contradiction upon him too, but the remark carries a sexual innuendo — 'if you lie in bed I'll make love to you'.
wife, spouse A superb indictment of the *habits* of the married state.
Hyde Park i.e. the resort for a parade of town fashion.
chariot i.e. carriage.
interrogatories Questions being asked.
articles subscribed i.e. rules obeyed.
bill of fare ... latter account The image is that of a meal menu, and the payment — or, the courses set for the banquet of marriage, the payment being the rules laid down.
enlarged into Sexual innuendo, plus the hope by Mirabell that he won't become the conventional husband.
Imprimis First of all.
covenant I decree, I lay it down that.
to screen her affairs under your countenance i.e. to hide her secret love affairs with your blessing.
No decoy-duck to wheedle you a fop No 'friend' to lead you secretly into the presence of an idle man of fashion.
the frolic which you had i.e. the game you were playing to test my fidelity to you.
I article i.e. I lay it down as a condition.
current i.e. in my favour.
new coin it i.e. change it into something different.
vizards Masks.
oiled-skins ... roasted cat Apparently this revolting catalogue is of the ingredients used in the preparation of cosmetics.
commerce i.e. social intercourse.
Item i.e. first on my list, next etc.
Odious endeavours! But the exclamation mark indicates how much she hopes to enjoy them.
strait-lacing Tight corseting.

a crooked billet A bent stick.
proviso The key word in this scene – the laying down of conditions for a real marriage and not the fashionable mockery of one.
toast fellows i.e. drink a toast to any men.
foreign forces Alien influences.
aniseed ... ratafia Strongly flavoured liqueurs. (See note p.27.)
clary Alcoholic drink that was made from honey and the herb clary, with pepper and ginger.
dormitives i.e. producing sleep, sedatives.
tractable Kind and obedient.
O horrid provisoes But she accepts them!
contract ... sealing of the deed Note the ironic use of this image, which is reflected far more seriously in other parts of the plot – with Fainall and Mrs Marwood particularly, and initially with 'Sir Rowland' and Lady Wishfort.

(Act 4, Scene 6)

I'll take my death i.e. I'm scared to death (that I shall accept him).
you have a mind to him You are very much attracted to him.
in a fair way i.e. likely to.
In the meantime i.e. I'll take it for granted that you have paid me a compliment.

(Act 4, Scene 7)

were upon i.e. were determined to (quarrel).
superannuated lubber i.e. too old bumpkin.

(Act 4, Scene 8)

like ten christenings i.e. because of the extent of the celebrations involved.
let out and pieced in the sides like an unsized camlet Like a garment which has not been stiffened; he is referring to his free and uncontrolled laughter.
composed i.e. made up.
Nolle prosequi A legal term – discontinuance of the case because the person bringing the prosecution does not wish to proceed.
like two roasting apples For Witwoud, a homely image.

(Act 4, Scene 9)

whim it about i.e. spin.
folios Large sheets.

decimo sexto A book based on 16 leaves (32 pages) to the basic sheet.
Lacedemonian Spartan. (One noted for bravery, hence ironic here.)
like a maker of pincushions (Dealing in remnants) because they are so small.
shorthand i.e. not understood.
Baldwin The ass in the story of *Reynard the Fox*, which is medieval in origin. By 'without a figure' he means 'not metaphorically speaking', that is, truthfully.
Gemini Twins; here used instead of 'a pair', 'a brace'. (Also, the third sign of the zodiac.)
mustard-seed Witwoud speaks figuratively – mustard-seed burns the tongue.
like a radish i.e. gives me wind.
gone together by the ears like a pair of castanets i.e. like hardwood instruments they would have clashed with one another.
less matters conclude premises i.e. smaller things give rise to arguments.
fight for your face i.e. to preserve yourself (both physical self and reputation is implied).
read romances A reference of contempt.
this pickle i.e. this state.

(Act 4, Scene 10)

Out upon't An expression of disgust.
comport yourself ... rantipole rate i.e. conduct yourself in this wild or reckless fashion.
Borachio Drunkard.
grutch i.e. begrudge.
laugh in my face i.e. bubbles and sparkles.
a bumper i.e. a full glass (of wine).
overtaken i.e. overcome.
In vino veritas After drinking wine, one speaks the truth.
piper ... dust it away ... t'other round i.e. I'll dance to the tune (of marriage); otherwise drop the idea, and let's have another song.
a good pimple i.e. a real friend.
soaker i.e. drinker.
Antipodes i.e. region opposite to our own.
Cousin, with the hard name i.e. Wit-woud (the pronunciation – and the pun that wood is hard).
let her keep her own counsel Keep her secret to herself.

cry out at the nine months' end In labour, when the child is born.
very powerful i.e. overpowering(ly) drunk.

(Act 4, Scene 11)

tallow-chandler One who made candles.
the Saracens Arabs or Moslems at the time of the Crusades.
Tartars Turks and Cossacks.
Turks i.e. from Turkey, known as fierce fighters.
infidels ... believe not in the grape A reference to the fact that Moslems are not allowed by their religion to drink any form of alcohol.
Mahometan, Mussulman Muslims.
stinkard i.e. a stinking person.
Mufti i.e. a Muslim priest.
Greek for claret i.e. language is nonsense, it's drink we want.
a fig for your Sultan and Sophy i.e. don't give a damn for these Eastern rulers.
tumbril i.e. cart full of dung.
sot i.e. drunkard.
bastinadoed Punished by being beaten on the soles of the feet.
an affair of moment Something of importance which I have to attend to immediately.
to all futurity For evermore.
cock-match i.e. cockfighting, a favourite sport of the time.
shakebag A game cock in the sport mentioned above.
bite your cheek i.e. kiss you.
breath like a bagpipe i.e. wheezy.
thy Pig i.e. associated with St Anthony.
never make a match i.e. with Millamant.

(Act 4, Scene 12)

the Pope distributes in the Year of Jubilee When the Pope pardons sins, originally at 100-year intervals but nowadays at 25-year intervals, during each Holy Year. (The year 1700 would certainly be a Jubilee Year, so this is a topical reference.)
severity of decorum i.e. constriction of conventional manners.
transport i.e. ecstasy.
tenter i.e. in suspense.
died away at my feet i.e. sworn that he would die if I did not return his love.
a'dies He shall die (for this).
an alms i.e. reduced to beg for his living.

a candle's end upon a saveall i.e. inserted in the candle to make sure that it burns out.
the clue i.e. the manner (to ensure that you achieve what you want).
appetite, or indigestion of widowhood i.e. not lust (though of course that is just what it is).
any lethargy of continence i.e. any failure on my part to maintain sexual self-control.
prone to any iteration of nuptials i.e. likely to repeat this performance (wish to be married).
recede ... prostitution of decorums i.e. withdraw ... abuse of proper behaviour.
fair shrine of virtue Waitwell plays up to what is needed – an excess of enthusiasm and romantic avowal.
least scruple of carnality Lady Wishfort protests too much – here she means 'the smallest jot of licentious desire'.
camphire and frankincense Camphor and incense (i.e. unsexual).
chastity and odour i.e. purity and sweetness (though there is an obvious play on the word 'odour'.)

(Act 4, Scene 13)

incessantly Constantly, unceasingly.

(Act 4, Scene 14)

cordial, I want spirits i.e. sustaining drink, for I am worn out (with having to pay court to Lady Wishfort).
to pant thus for i.e. to complain because ...
antidote Hardly a flattering way of describing how put off he is by Lady Wishfort.
no appetite to iteration of nuptials He is taking up Lady Wishfort's words and twisting them, implying that as a result of his attentions to Lady Wishfort, he will have no desire to make love to Foible.
chairman in the dog-days i.e. the carrier (or 'porter') of a sedan chair in July and August – the hottest days of the summer.

(Act 4, Scene 15)

superscription i.e. the superiority of the writing.
my heart aches i.e. with apprehension.
'tis from nobody that I know An underlining of the essential simplicity of Lady Wishfort.
you are abused i.e. being taken advantage of.

suborned for that imposure i.e. bribed to undertake this deception.
Roman hand Large round handwriting.
I'd pistol him i.e. shoot him.
this pearl of India i.e. this jewel (Lady Wishfort).
character Handwriting.
at this juncture At this point, moment.
was contriving i.e. was being secretly undertaken.
discompose you i.e. put you out, worry you.
his date is short His time is running out.
incur the law i.e. have action taken against you (for killing Mirabell).
I must never show my face i.e. because I would be the woman responsible for your death.
conjure i.e. beg.
writings of my whole estate i.e. the legal details.
happy discovery Fortunate revelation.
abandoned i.e. corrupt, licentious.
Or arrant knave Foible has the last telling aside to the audience – for she knows the truth.

Revision questions on Act 4

1 What elements of farce do you find in this act? Write an appreciation of the techniques used by Congreve to increase the *pace* of the play.

2 Write a character-sketch of Sir Wilfull Witwoud.

3 Write an appreciation of the parts played by Foible and Waitwell in this act.

4 Do you (or do you not) feel any sympathy for Lady Wishfort? You should refer closely to the text in your answer.

Act 5

The scene opens dramatically with (for Congreve) plenty of action, for Lady Wishfort is in the process of dismissing Foible. The latter tries to convince Lady Wishfort that she has acted in her employer's best interests, but fails to do so. Foible meets Mrs Fainall, and the two agree that Mrs Marwood and Fainall are responsible for the present situation. Foible reveals to Mrs Fainall that Mrs Marwood is her husband's mistress. Meanwhile Lady Wishfort thanks Mrs Marwood for saving her, and then turns on her daughter, who in return tells her how *she* has been abused. When Mrs Fainall leaves, Mrs Marwood points out that Lady Wishfort runs the risk of being exposed in court (over 'Sir Rowland', for example). Then Fainall comes to make his demands; apart from matters of money and estate, he tells Lady Wishfort that she may not marry. While the papers are being drawn up, Sir Wilfull appears with Millamant, according to plan, saying that he wishes to marry her. Mirabell makes his abject apologies to Lady Wishfort, and Fainall reappears to make his final demands. Mirabell says that he can yet save Lady Wishfort, who promises him Millamant – despite her nephew! – if he does so. Foible and Mincing give evidence of Mrs Marwood's affair with Fainall; Sir Rowland appears with the black box; and Mirabell reveals how he had safeguarded Mrs Fainall from Fainall's mercenary designs even before she was married to him. In the last scene all is revealed, reconciliation being the theme – though Fainall has left in anger.

Initially it is the passionate rejection of Foible by Lady Wishfort which provides the action: the abuse is extreme and reveals the ways of the outside world. It shows the social divisions between the classes very clearly. Foible almost makes things worse by her confession, for it is clear that she and Waitwell (and of course Mirabell) have used and abused Lady Wishfort. Note the range of the latter's rhetorical verve and the imagery of her vituperation. The play on bride and Bridewell is effectively funny even in this context. But with Lady Wishfort off stage the Mirabell plot comes into its own with Mrs Fainall comforting Foible by revealing Mirabell's action on Waitwell's behalf. Foible's own dramatic stroke is to reveal Fainall's affair with Mrs Marwood, though we note her hypocrisy over the swearing of the oath to Marwood – as long as it wasn't sworn on the Bible it can readily be broken. Country and town contrast reappears with the ridiculous wish of Lady Wishfort's that she and Marwood should become shepherdesses (Congreve obviously mocking the pastoral and fake pastoral conventions), but the best irony is employed when Lady Wishfort gives an account of the repressive education of her daughter. This was calculated to keep her pure, a laughable standpoint when we think of Lady Wishfort's own licentious nature. Marwood's blackmailing response to this is to throw the fear of the law and the publicity which attends exposure at Lady Wishfort. The action of the scene now consists of the exposure of Fainall after his own blackmailing procedures. The first step is the declaration of Millamant that she will have Sir Wilfull. This is mimicry of the marriage of convenience. Marwood realizes that the power of Mirabell is asserting itself. And Mirabell's own confession is tellingly made, the reaction, to use her own image, 'rakes the embers' in Lady Wishfort's breast. Fainall uses much bravado to no avail, his defeat shows the way of the world of justice operating against him. Notice how Mirabell directs the action, almost producing the denouement of this final sequence himself. (As Witwoud puts it, 'are you all got together, like players at the end of the last act?') Fainall and Marwood, the agents of chaos, are both defeated by the prevision of Mirabell. Sir Wilfull demonstrates his own generosity of spirit. The final couplets of the play contain the moral comment on the action – marital deception and infidelity breeds the like. That is the way of the world.

(Act 5, Scene 1)

bosom traitress i.e. betrayed by someone trusted.
weaving of dead hair i.e. making wigs.
chafing-dish It held charcoal, and thus heated anything put on it. This description indicates that Lady Wishfort raised Foible from the meanest of servant employment.
traverse rag i.e. a curtain used as a screen – again indicative of poverty.
drive a trade i.e. make a living.
flaunting upon a packthread Hanging showily on thick rope.
bulk Stall.
dead wall i.e. a wall that had no breaks in it.
ballad-monger Seller of (street) songs.
frisoneer-gorget A woollen neckerchief.
colberteen This was French lace of a cheap variety.
commodities i.e. wares.
governante Housekeeper.
seduced me i.e. won me over.

the wealth of the Indies The East and West Indies are referred to (known for silks, spices etc.).
a cast serving-man i.e. a sacked servant.
receptacle i.e. to be used.
a decayed pimp An ageing procurer.
frontless i.e. without shame.
a big-bellied actress i.e. one that is pregnant.
to secure In order to obtain.
put upon his clergy A literate offender could claim 'benefit of clergy', a privilege once extended to clergymen, and thus escape the death sentence.
meddle or make i.e. have anything to do with it.
broker i.e. acting on your behalf.
a passive bawd i.e. an inactive procuress.
botcher of second-hand marriages A bad repairer of grubby marriages between maids and manservants (Abigails and Andrews); these names are apparently derived from those of servants in two of Beaumont and Fletcher's plays.
baste Stitch together, tack.
Philander Lover.
a Bridewell-bride Bridewell was the prison for women offenders, where they were forced to work.

(Act 5, Scene 2)

be had i.e. be taken.
give security i.e. put up security, offer bail.
missing effect i.e. failing to achieve the result.
to go for the papers i.e. his estate papers in the black box.
confederacy i.e. conspiracy.
stifled i.e. stopped any further reading.
our living together With Fainall, as man and wife.
he has been even with your ladyship He too has had an affair.
set 'em at distance i.e. make them distant with one another.
a fair word i.e. a hint (and bribery perhaps) to keep quiet.
a safe conscience Easy in our own minds.

(Act 5, Scene 3)

your spouse i.e. Waitwell.
perilous passion i.e. fearful temper.
to vouch i.e. testify the truth of what I say.
be what it will i.e. whatever it is (Mincing, of course, has no regard for the truth).

(Act 5, Scene 4)

intercessor i.e. intervening to help.
compound for the frailties of my daughter i.e. settle, make up for the weaknesses of my daughter (Mrs Fainall).
groves and purling streams Congreve is mocking the pastoral convention and the affectation of a return to nature of those who are in fact dependent on 'fashion' and the artificial life.
the treaty i.e. the agreement.
most minute particle of severe virtue i.e. the strict bounds of propriety and convention.
mould ... pattern ... model Ironic terms, in view of Lady Wishfort's 'appetite' at this stage in her life.
naught i.e. naughty, in the sense of immorality, misbehaviour.
to compound your caprices and your cuckoldoms To make up for your whims and the betrayal of your husband.
sophisticated False.
My friend The word carries sexual implications in this context.
temper A (more) moderate tone.
misconstruction i.e. misinterpretation.
returns i.e. rewards for your service to me.
she'll drop off when she's full i.e. when she has robbed you (leeches drop off when they have absorbed a surfeit of blood).
bodkin A long pointless needle used for drawing tape, elastic etc. through hems; a long pin for fastening the hair.
brass counter A small (usually round) piece used in card or other games. (These 'counters' can also be made of ivory, plastic or metals other than brass.)
aspersions Unfair accusations.

(Act 5, Scene 5)

unexceptionable i.e. exemplary.
a young odium and aversion i.e. caused her to hate the male sex. (Lady Wishfort is unaware of the psychological damage she may have done, and this is part of the humour.)
though but in coats Even if he were in long clothes.
babies Dolls.
and him we made a shift i.e. we forced him to pretend.
going in Nearly.
'Twas much i.e. it was some achievement.
catechized i.e. allowed him to hear her catechism.
profane music-meetings Lady Wishfort is puritanical about the evils of music.
excommunication i.e. that she would be expelled from the church.

prostituted i.e. wantonly used.
a pack of bawling lawyers Note the effect of the animal imagery – almost as if the defendant is to be attacked (as indeed she is, verbally).
O Yes Hear ye (the phrase used by the town-criers of the time to obtain silence; 'Oyez' is the best-known version of this cry).
old fumbling lecher (Penguin edition 'old fumbling lecher') i.e. a dirty old man.
in a coif like a man midwife In the white cap (part of the legal dress of the serjeant-at-law) who will probe, deliver you of your secrets.
infamy Guilt.
by the statute According to the law. She will be made a permanent joke or mockery for the lawyers.
Domesday-book The record of the land-survey carried out in 1085–6, during the reign of William the Conqueror.
naughty interrogatories ... naughty Law Latin i.e. degrading questions ... more degrading and debased Latin.
cantharides i.e. dried beetles, were used for raising blisters in order to treat various ailments; also as a diuretic and an aphrodisiac.
cow-itch Cowhage, a tropical plant with pods covered in stinging hairs.
revellers of the Temple i.e. law students living riotously.
like prentices at a conventicle Those youths bound to dissenting tradesmen who had to take down what was said in the sermons they attended, so that they could give an account to their masters.
in Commons The meal served in the dining-hall.
flounderman's Apparently based on a real seller of fish. The man had a loud, cleverly varied voice.
stunned i.e. bemused, overcome.
insupportable i.e. insufferable, intolerable.
I'll compound I'll come to terms.
composition i.e. agreement.
overseen i.e. overlooked.
huddle up i.e. hush up.

(Act 5, Scene 6)

importunity Pressure.
when we retire to our pastoral solitude Mrs Marwood is being ironic, the back-to-nature theme being part of the affectation of the time.
in case of necessity It may be necessary that I marry for my own good.

prescribed i.e. the idea is of a doctor prescribing a cure – heavy irony from Fainall.
physic ... apothecary Medicine ... from the druggist.
Muscovite Russian.
Czarish Majesty's retinue Those attending on the Czar, Peter the Great, when he visited England in the 1790s.
in right of i.e. because of the existence of.
non compos Not capable, not in his senses (he was drunk).
instrument is drawing i.e. while the agreement is being prepared.
till more sufficient deeds i.e. until a complete (not an interim) legal agreement can be drawn up.
may balance this matter i.e. weigh up this situation (in your own mind).

(Act 5, Scene 7)

be subject to i.e. be ruled by.
smart i.e. suffer.
though her year was not out i.e. although she hadn't been a widow for a full year.
matched now with a witness i.e. she has got what she deserved (in marrying Fainall).
to be confiscated at this rebel-rate i.e. to be sacrificed to this high-handed man.
two more of my Egyptian plagues See Exodus, Chapters 7–12 for the plagues suffered by Pharaoh.

(Act 5, Scene 8)

caterpillar You vile person.
in disguise i.e. not myself, drunk.
to make satisfaction i.e. make reparation (for it).
an it cost i.e. even if it cost.
flower of knighthood A deliberate affectation (which indicates to the audience how insincere she is).
without i.e. outside.
fortify myself to support his appearance i.e. brace myself to endure the sight of him.
as a Gorgon One of three sisters in Greek mythology who had the power of turning to stone anyone who looked directly at them.
Pylades and Orestes Close friends in the Greek story of Orestes' revenge for his father's death; Pylades helped him to kill Clytemnestra and Aegisthus.

68 The Way of the World

proviso The significant word, here used in low key, and meaning 'on the condition that'.
will cross 'em i.e. the seas.
who'll hinder him i.e. stop him.
precious fooling i.e. there is something going on, but I'll find out about it.

(Act 5, Scene 10)

instrument i.e. agreement.
That sham is too gross i.e. that bluff is too obvious.
my pretensions i.e. my claims.
old fox i.e. a sword.
ram vellum i.e. the parchment of the agreement.
Mittimus A warrant.
tailor's measure These too were sometimes made of parchment.
respite Contain, control.
beef-eater i.e. one of the guards of the Tower of London.
as pursuant ... this other covenant i.e. as related to the argument and conditions of the other agreement.
not requisite Not essential.
make a bear-garden flourish The reference is to bear-baiting and the fights between spectators that went on outside the pit.
like a leaky hulk The image is crudely effective.
But that you would not I realize that you would not let me help you.
disposed of her i.e. of Millamant (to Sir Wilfull).
I'll break my nephew's match i.e. I'll break if off, stop it.
and a penitent i.e. she comes to beg your pardon.

(Act 5, Scene 11)

these corrupt things i.e. Foible and Waitwell.
it's but the Way of the World Fainall's cynical statement means: what must happen must happen; there's no stopping it.
one tittle i.e. the smallest amount.
to give credit i.e. accept the word of.
Messalina's poems An apt choice, since the Empress Messalina (died AD 48), wife of the Roman emperor Claudius (10 BC–AD 54), was licentious and cruel. But Mincing's affectation is such that most editors take the view that she meant 'miscellaneous' poems.
smart i.e. suffer.
wherewithal i.e. sufficient money or clothing.
a groat A coin to the (then) value of fourpence (about 1.8 new pence).

(Act 5, Scene 12)

At hand i.e. nearby.
I'll not wait I won't hang about for your private business.

(Act 5, Scene 13)

whose hand's out? Who is creating trouble?
like players at the end of the last act Wit, since Congreve is laughing at himself and his own 'play'.
your hands i.e. signatures as witnesses.
hand ... mark The implication is that Petulant cannot write, that he is illiterate and has to sign with his 'mark'.
while she was at her own disposal i.e. while she had control of her own decisions.
pretended i.e. fake.
partial opinion i.e. biased viewpoint.
sages learned in the laws of this land i.e. lawyers.
serve your occasions i.e. tell you all you want to know.
A Deed of Conveyance i.e. making over to.
'tis the Way of the World A deliberate and ironic echo by Mirabell of Fainall's own words.
elder Earlier.
you may make your bear-garden Sir Wilfull is not without 'wit', as he shows here by also echoing Fainall's words.
vent Freedom.

(Act 5, Scene 14)

prudence i.e. caution.
engaged a volunteer in this action i.e. offered to help us himself in this situation.
designs to prosecute his travels i.e. to undertake his trip abroad.
off or on Either way, it's all the same to me.
like a dog in a dancing school i.e. turning this way and that to follow the dancers.
I would have you as often Even at this juncture, Mirabell cannot resist the sexual innuendo.
toy i.e. dote (on each other) with hand-kissing etc.
disquiet not yourself i.e. don't you worry.
of force comply i.e. he'll have to agree.
a reunion i.e. between Fainall and Mrs Fainall.
too oft are paid in kind i.e. returned, tit for tat.

Revision questions on Act 5

1 Write an account of Mirabell's plot to forestall Fainall in his designs.

2 Write an essay in appreciation of Congreve's ability to unravel the plot successfully in this act.

3 Estimate the part played by Sir Wilfull and Lady Wishfort in the *humour* of this act.

4 What does this act tell you of Congreve's attitude towards human nature?

Epilogue

doom its fall i.e. pronounce judgement on it.
their number's swell'd i.e. there are many bad poets.
judging in the pit i.e. making their comments and notes close to the stage.
who by characters are meant i.e. what and who the characters in the play represent.
the copied face The original on whom the character is based
glosses Explanatory notes (like these textual notes).
libel ... satire i.e. get the author into trouble by distorting his object.
the fools design'd i.e. the critics may discover that they are the very ones satirized in the play.
abstracted i.e. separated (satire would not stoop to take notice of one of these fops).
So poets oft Playwrights often in one play reveal a mixed bag of fashionable gatherings.

The characters

Millamant

'Here she comes i' faith full sail, with her fan spread and streamers out, and a shoal of fools for tenders ...'

Millamant's entrance, described above, is well into the second act, but she immediately makes an impact. She is lively and vivacious, able to mock the kind of society in which she moves, and is particularly severe on what today would be called male chauvinism. She recoils from illiteracy and this reflects her need of stimulating conversation. She treats the idea of marriage seriously, not as just a fashionable game. She stands out from the other female characters because of her cultured range of references and her views on marriage. She represents the reality beneath appearances; she has a lively apprehension of what marriage can become and understands that mutual respect and independence are its essential ingredients.

Millamant has a natural ease of utterance, and her wit and understanding of the way of her world are immediately apparent. As she says, 'one makes lovers as fast as one pleases ... and they die as soon as one pleases: and then if one pleases one makes more.' She sees through Witwoud but tolerates him – though it is a tolerance expressive of contempt. She ridicules those who would pay false court to her; and her satirical turns involve condemnation of people who write too many letters (particularly in verse). She affects to be cruel ('I love to give pain'), but we doubt her honesty here, just as Mirabell does. Her serious consideration of marriage is in part tempered by her fears of what she would give up, for she feels that it is 'so tedious to be told of one's faults'. Although she realizes that she is attracted by Mirabell she is delightfully satirical at his expense (we sympathize with her in this), when she says 'Sententious Mirabell! Prithee don't look with that violent and inflexible wise face.' She is clever enough to reveal to him that she is aware of his plot with Foible and Waitwell, and in a sense this anticipates her determination to love but *not* to be subordinate, or to be treated one jot less respectfully than her chosen man. Millamant does not often dominate or command the stage, and is absent for most of the third act; but halfway through the act she does have a telling encounter with Marwood, which begins innocently enough with Millamant condemning the contradictions of Petulant. Mrs Marwood, however, tells her that 'the town has found it', referring to her affair with Mirabell. But Millamant, in splendid raillery, puts Mrs Marwood in her place ('I think you are handsomer – and within a year or two as young'), following this with a song whose innuendo is certainly a reflection of her own triumph with Mirabell and of Marwood's failure.

Millamant is delightfully undecided in Act 4 whether or not to see Mirabell, though we suspect she knows that she must; in the next scene we find her quoting Suckling, then Waller; having despatched Sir Wilfull, she entertains Mirabell, has her quotation capped and considers losing her liberty and her (supposed) solitude. Her indictment of fashionable marriage behaviour ('as if we were proud of one another the first week, and ashamed of one another ever after') gives way to an account of her own intentions should she submit to that state, when she will 'Come to dinner when I please, dine in my dressing-room when I'm out of humour, without giving a reason. To have my closet inviolate; to be sole empress of my tea-table, which you must never presume to approach without first asking leave'. She enlarges on the theme of the hypocrisy of society; and her final acceptance of Mirabell is a delicious example of her 'shall I – shan't I' vacillation. Yet when she talks to Mrs Fainall afterwards, her self-acknowledgment ('for I find I love him violently') is one of the most moving moments in the play.

From this point, Millamant takes little direct part in the action. She is disgusted with Sir Wilfull's drunkenness, and leaves. Admittedly she helps in the plot that Mirabell has devised, pretending that she and Sir Wilfull are betrothed; and there is little doubt that she relishes the humour of the situation and the duplicity involved. Her last words in the play underline her gift for the double-entendre, and her positive sexuality – as distinct from the role-playing of her contemporaries. She says, 'Why does not the man take me? Would you have me give myself to you over again?' She is attractive, fluent, sharp and entertaining, full of the spice of innuendo that hides a genuine wish to love and to be loved for herself.

Mirabell

'I have been engaged in a matter of some sort of mirth, which is not yet ripe for discovery.'

Mirabell is a fashionable man-about-town, one who has been something of a rake but who has come to recognize that the love of his life is unquestionably Millamant. He is a truewit, a turner of phrases ('I happen to be grave today; and you are gay'), his antithetical sentences reflecting the contrasting elements in his own character. Much of his personality, including his love for Millamant, is revealed in the first scene in the play when he and Fainall exchange pleasantries: in Fainall's case, searching ones.

Mirabell is a plotter. His initial scheme was to make advances to Lady Wishfort so that he could pay real court to Millamant. This uncovered, he now intends to compromise Lady Wishfort by having her contracted to his pretended uncle, Sir Rowland, who is really his servant Waitwell in disguise. Since Waitwell has already married Foible, Mirabell shrewdly hopes to grasp the opportunity of pledging his silence in order to avoid scandal, thereby securing Lady Wishfort's consent to his marriage with Millamant. He is wary of Fainall, yet confesses to him: 'I like her with all her faults; nay, like her for her faults ... They are now grown as familiar to me as my own frailties; and in all probability in a little time longer I shall like 'em as well'.

Mirabell is a great one for word-play and punning (note the remark that the half-brother Sir Willfull 'may be but half a fool'), and he delights in baiting Witwoud. Still we feel that Mirabell is serious beneath the verbal froth, for he questions others searchingly about Millamant's behaviour and feelings. In the past he has had an affair with Mrs Fainall; suspicious of Fainall, Mirabell rescues her from his machinations by having her estate made over to himself. This demonstrates his capacity for opportunism, too, since we know that his motives involve not only saving Mrs Fainall, but also getting on the right side of Lady Wishfort. Yet he trusts Mrs Fainall sufficiently to reveal the whole plot to her, so that we are convinced he is working towards the right ends. He is incapable of understanding Millamant's tolerance of fools like Witwoud and Petulant ('for sure to please a fool is some degree of folly'), but this can in part be put down to jealousy – they spend so much time in Millamant's company. He speaks of winning Millamant 'with plain-dealing and sincerity'. In fact, his emotions are divulged in a remarkable soliloquy that reveals the man himself: he says of women, 'for motion not method is their occupation. To know this, and yet continue to be in love, is to be made wise from the dictates of reason, and yet persevere to play the fool by the force of instinct'.

Mirabell is absent from Act 3, but the celebrated 'proviso' scene dominates Act 4. The exchanges of the two lovers balance one another verbally, just as the two characters respond to each other emotionally – and they penetrate to the heart of the real matter of marriage rather than just to the sophisticated toy it has become. Mirabell has his own contempt for the conventions of society and is audacious enough to give orders to Millamant regarding what she may and may not do 'when you shall be breeding' (though she counters here with spirited rejoinders); he then enters a number of provisos which damn the practices of society ladies ('mending of fashions, spoiling reputations, railing at absent friends') which he will permit, while forbidding 'strait-lacing' (to control the figure), licentious behaviour or drinking.

Again Mirabell disappears from the scene, but he is not idle. He returns, having supposedly bequeathed Millamant to Sir Wilfull, obviously enjoys apologizing to Lady Wishfort and then takes the means of redress into his own hands. His reply to Fainall, which reveals that he (Mirabell) holds the deeds of Mrs Fainall's estate, underlines the title and gives it an ironic twist – 'Even so, sir, 'tis the Way of the World, sir: of the widows of the world.' At the very end he reveals that he is motivated not just by his own affairs. His own marriage is now to be made, but he is intent, too, on mending that between Fainall and Mrs Fainall, 'to make you live easily together'.

Mirabell is not a cynical man of fashion but he is forced to employ deception to achieve his ends, based as they are on a recognition of what is real, and a rejection of the fashionable ways of the world.

Fainall

'Well, sure if I could live to be rid of my wife, I should be a miserable man.'

Fainall, like his mistress, Marwood, is thoroughly unscrupulous and accordingly stands in diametric contrast to Mirabell. He spends much of his time testing, for example employing raillery against Mirabell in their opening verbal encounter, and trying to elicit his feelings for Millamant. Yet he is not without wit, and fulfils an important function in the plot, for he talks of Mirabell's past advances to Lady Wishfort and is amusing at the expense of the Cabal-nights of the ladies (and Witwoud and Petulant). His name, like that of Mrs Marwood, is a splendid character give-away ('I fain – I would like – all') and ('mar everything – I would').

Fainall's first testing of Mirabell is followed by his testing of his mistress. With characteristic wit he urges Mirabell to marry Millamant ('be half as well acquainted with her charms as you are with her defects'), and he is particularly fluent and colourful when talking of Sir Wilfull and Witwoud. But it *is* talk, and his life is spent in chocolate houses, playing cards and assessing how best to retain both his mistress and his wife's fortune. Fainall represents greed and selfishness, and the beginning of Act 2 finds him involved in a particularly ugly exchange with Mrs Marwood – ugly because it highlights his falseness, jealousy and lack of caring. This scene should be read in conjunction with Mirabell's exchange with Millamant in Act 4, where the truth of relationships and the falsehoods of fashionable life are fully related. Fainall ask Mrs Marwood, 'But could you think, because the nodding husband would not wake, that e'er the watchful lover slept?' He is incensed at the thought of being betrayed ('and wherefore did I marry, but to make lawful prize of a rich widow's wealth, and squander it on love and you?' However, he needs Marwood and she needs him; he tells her once more that he loves her, declaring, 'I'll hate my wife yet more, damn her.'

Congreve's practice is to switch the focus of the playgoer's interest and Fainall does not reappear until the end of the third act. There we find him ranting about being 'cuckolded' by his wife with Mirabell – further evidence that his 'rank-wife', as he calls her, cannot be permitted the degree of licence he regards as natural for himself. He falls in unscrupulously with Marwood's suggestion that they should disclose Mrs Fainall's adultery to Lady Wishfort, and thus obtain Mrs Fainall's estate. Fainall vows, 'I'll turn my wife to grass', and launches into a bitter attack on the state of being married (again, compare with Mirabell and Millamant), saying of husbands, 'I am single, and will herd no more with 'em. True, I wear the badge, but I'll disown the order. And since I take my leave of 'em, I care not if I leave 'em a common motto to their common crest'. The plan seemingly works well, with Fainall confronting Lady Wishfort, forbidding her to marry, and sadistically enjoying his exercise of power. Outmanoeuvred by Mirabell, Fainall threatens to assault his wife, and warns Mirabell that he will 'hear of this'. Mirabell's optimism that the marriage may be saved hardly seems justified, for Fainall, like his mistress, represents the black side of Restoration comedy.

Mrs Marwood

'But for the discovery of this amour, I am indebted to your friend, or your wife's friend, Mrs Marwood.'

The 'black' aspect of the play is further emphasized in the character of Mrs Marwood, who complements Fainall at every turn. Her character is largely built upon jealousy, since she is attracted by Mirabell. As Fainall observes to Mirabell, 'Women do not easily forgive omissions of that nature', for he feels that Mrs Marwood may have been slighted by Mirabell. Mrs Marwood is an intriguer, gaining the ear of Lady Wishfort and urging Fainall to a course of action that will ensure he gets Mrs Fainall's estate. Her motive is revenge; but she is observant, noting Foible's meeting with Mirabell: and she is adept at uncovering plots and laying or initiating her own.

We first meet her at the beginning of Act 2, talking to Mrs Fainall; she reveals that she pretends to hate men in order to be free to do what she wants. As Mrs Fainall observes, 'you profess a libertine', and it is here – in the area of freedom of action that we may contrast Mrs Marwood with Millamant. In the latter's case the freedom is of rational action, but in Mrs Marwood's it is the freedom of licence; yet Mrs Marwood has a certain power, the power of persuasion. She returns to her theme of hatred of mankind, but says that she would like to carry it further by actually marrying (in order to be revenged). Again the contrast with Millamant's motivation is displayed. Her exchange with Fainall, who has detected her partiality for Mirabell, demonstrates the bitterness of which she is capable; she says, as he tries to hold her hands, 'I'd leave 'em to get loose', and this is the strongest language used in the play. One understands her anger, for she has trusted Fainall with her fortune and, perhaps more important, her reputation. She hides in the closet while Lady Wishfort interrogates Foible, and afterwards indulges in a soliloquy redolent of bitterness: 'Man, Man! Woman, Woman! The devil's an ass: if I were a painter, I would draw him like an idiot, a driveller with a bib and bells. Man should have his head and horns, and woman the rest of him'. She is critical of society too, but it is a mordant humour, as Millamant notes.

Mrs Marwood unfortunately reveals inadvertently what she feels for Mirabell, and is then humbled by the wit and innuendo of Millamant. She goes a long way towards humouring Sir Wilfull on his meeting with his half-brother, and then sets up Fainall's plot to get his wife's estate by revealing Mrs Fainall's previous adultery with Mirabell. She contrives the letter to Lady Wishfort exposing Sir Rowland, though Foible manages to reduce, indeed deflect, its impact. Although she has asserted 'I can play the incendiary', we may note that she is 'damped' by Mirabell's counter-plan. She is absent from the action of Act 4, but returns in Act 5 to acquaint Lady Wishfort with her daughter's crime, directing her to the practical business in hand; as Mrs Fainall observes, 'I tell you, madam, you're abused. – Stick to you? Ay, like a leech, to suck your best blood – she'll drop off when she's full'. Marwood is not finished, and further underlines what it will be like for Lady Wishfort to have her name 'prostituted in a public court'. She shows herself possessed of considerable irony when she reminds Lady Wishfort that 'when we retire to our pastoral solitude we shall bid adieu to all other thoughts'. Her last words are a vicious assertion that she will 'perish in the attempt' to bring Mrs Fainall's reputation down. She may be contrasted with Millamant at every turn, for she represents the immoral, intriguing, licentious facet of fashionable society at its worst.

Lady Wishfort

'Full of the vigour of fifty-five, declares for a friend and ratafia; and let posterity shift for itself, she'll breed no more.'

Lady Wishfort first appears at the opening of Act 3, and from then on is one of the main focuses of interest in the play. Her language (see Meredith's quote in the section on *Style*) is colourful and often coarse, and she has a vast range of images with which to reinforce its natural power, since she is a great talker. She is gullible, an easy prey to the machinations of Mrs Marwood, who tells her what Mirabell has said of her, thus occasioning the extreme remark from Lady Wishfort, 'I'll marry a drawer to have him poisoned in his wine.' She is lustful, badly wanting marriage, but always mindful of her reputation and the need to preserve 'decorums'. In a serious character this could be called hypocrisy; but with Lady Wishfort one feels that, despite her strong language, she is not possessed of sufficient malice to do injury, or of sufficient independence to be uninfluenced by others.

Lady Wishfort can be forthrightly honest ('I am arrantly flayed'), but her sexual appetite is such that she concentrates too on the effect she will create in support of the picture Foible has shown 'Sir Rowland' ('a little scorn is alluring'). She is disgusted with Sir Wilfull when he gets drunk ('he would poison a tallow-chandler and his family'), but her treatment of 'Sir Rowland' shows that the rehearsals cannot overcome her sense of propriety, misguided though it is; she tells him, 'you must not attribute my yielding to any sinister appetite, or indigestion of widowhood; nor impute my complacency to any lethargy of continence – I hope you do not think me prone to any iteration of nuptials'. The reverse is so obviously the truth that it makes her a figure of fun, but a sympathetic one.

The delivery of the letter shows how easily influenced Lady Wishfort is. She begs 'Sir Rowland' not to act, and to value her reputation; but her most voluble abuse is saved for Foible ('O thou frontless impudence, more than a big-bellied actress'). Nevertheless, she is swayed by Marwood to 'leave the world, and retire by ourselves and be shepherdesses'. Through her, Congreve satirizes the impractical affectation of back-to-nature of the period.

When condemning her daughter, Lady Wishfort indulges in new flights of alliterative rhetoric: 'Here I am ruined to compound for your caprices and your cuckoldoms.' But her account of how she brought her daughter up ('aversion to the very sight of men') proves how wholly misguided she has been. She remains susceptible to Mirabell ('Oh, he has witchcraft in his eyes and tongue'), and consents at once to his match with Millamant when it is obvious that he can save her reputation. He also says he will protect her from any 'desperate course' undertaken by Fainall. Lady Wishfort is grotesque, but rich in the life of the author's imagination.

Witwoud

'Friendship without freedom is as dull as love without enjoyment, or wine without toasting.'

Witwoud's name underlines his limitations – he would be a wit, and indeed keeps a commonplace-book in which he writes down his 'similitudes', which he cunningly (and often falsely) introduces into the conversation. He is a follower of Millamant's, that is, he is seen in her company and in the company of the ladies at their Cabal-nights.

Not only is Witwoud the other half of a music-hall act with Petulant, he is also only half-committed to anything. He would like to be thought a full man-about-town – in reality he is only half a one. His conversation is entirely directed towards making an impression; and he considers himself very hard done by when he learns that his half-brother, Sir Wilfull, is coming to town. Before that, he undertakes a masterly 'damning with faint praise' of his 'friend' Petulant; as he says, 'His want of learning gives him the more opportunities to show his natural parts'. His lack of sincerity or commitment is based on the fear of losing what he now enjoys: a reputation. He tells Fainall that Millamant is 'a sort of an uncertain woman ... she's a woman and a kind of humourist.' Millamant urges him to spare the company his similitudes, but Witwoud is always set fair on this particular verbal course.

Witwoud's affectations offend his brother when that worthy country gentleman eventually appears. Society's lack of breeding is reflected in Witwoud's own bad taste and his acute snobbery ('this fellow would have bound me to a maker of felts'). The next time we see him he is somewhat drunk but still capable of baiting Petulant. He also encourages Sir Wilfull in his own drunkenness. Witwoud is virtually absent from Act 5 (apart from testifying that he has witnessed the making over of Mrs Fainall's estate to Mirabell), and is a good example of the superficial parasitic man of fashion with no underlying morality or sense of the truth to make him more than half a man.

Petulant

'where he would send in for himself, what I mean, call for himself, wait for himself, nay and what's more, not finding himself, sometimes leave a letter for himself.'

Petulant is not nearly as fully developed as Witwoud, but he too is admirably named. He affects to be annoyed at having the three ladies call upon him and acts as a gossip, retailing to Mirabell his own fabricated news about his uncle. He is strong in contradiction, but stronger in cowardice. Discretion is certainly the better part of his valour ('If throats are to be cut, let swords clash; snug's the word, I shrug and am silent'). He has a certain degree of wit himself ('Beg him for his estate; that I may beg you afterwards'). His main theme is against learning, for he does not consider it necessary to either love-making or marriage. He joins in the baiting of Sir Wilfull, delighted to discover that Witwoud was once an attorney's clerk. In his drunkenness he is still coarsely witty ('go flea dogs and read romances – I'll go to bed to my maid'), and occasionally accurate ('Witwoud – you are an annihilator of phrases'). He doesn't write, he doesn't read, and is merely another parasite living off the fashionable world.

Sir Wilfull Witwoud

'But when he's drunk, he's as loving as the monster in *The Tempest*; and much after the same manner.'

Fainall's words prove to be true, but to be fair he has also said that Sir Wilfull is 'an odd mixture of bashfulness and obstinacy'. Sir Wilfull's first entrance is towards the end of Act 3, and he disturbs the idle fashionable world by the time of his arrival ('we should count it towards afternoon in our parts, down in Shropshire'). He recognizes his brother and, without satirical intention, describes him for what he is, 'so becravated and so beperriwigged'. He rightly takes offence at the superior affectations of Witwoud, and very effectively calls a spade a spade by revealing unwelcome details of his brother's past.

Sir Wilfull is set upon travelling abroad; but before that he tries to pluck up courage – via a bottle or two – to propose to Millamant, in accordance with his aunt's wishes. But he cannot bring himself to do so, becomes thoroughly drunk and offends Lady Wishfort and Millamant in the process – though there is a certain coarse and entertaining humour in his antics. He becomes a 'fellow-traveller' of Mirabell's and, as part of the plot, affects to be engaged to Millamant; he also prepares to defend Lady Wishfort against Fainall, and at least gets his revenge verbally on that vicious character. He is likeable, unattractive but with a rightness of feeling, his own honesty contrasting with the general falseness of the town.

Other characters

Mrs Fainall is a pathetic character. Having been widowed, she marries for the second time and discovers that her foppish husband covets her estate. She has had an affair with Mirabell in the past, and trusts him to protect her against her husband should the latter prove unscrupulous, which he does. She sees through Marwood, and during her talk with Mirabell learns the nature of his plot. She is sympathetic and good, but in a muted way.

Waitwell and *Foible* are a delight; they deserve each other, for they have an eye to the main chance, are cunning but likeable, and are essential to the unravelling of the plot. Foible indeed is intelligently devious; managing to win Lady Wishfort back from Marwood. Waitwell's impersonation of 'Sir Rowland' indicates that he will be somewhat wasted on the farm which Mirabell is to provide for the happy couple.

Mincing lives only through her speech, which is memorable, her affected gentility matching the equally cheap affectations of some of her superiors.

Structure and style

Structure

Congreve is a master of form. The first act reveals Mirabell's plot, takes a side look at Witwoud and Petulant and builds up a considerable amount of interest in Millamant before she appears in Act 2. At the beginning of Act 2 there is clever duplication, to point a contrast, with Mrs Fainall and Mrs Marwood cast in almost the same kind of exchange as Mirabell and Fainall in Act 1 – as though we are being given an insight into good and bad, by turns. With the movement of this act comes the revelation of the Fainall – Mrs Marwood intrigue, then the fine exchanges between Mirabell and Millamant. The contrast and balance is almost diagrammatic, with two supplying the tension, and others providing a look at society. There is a switch in Act 3 to Lady Wishfort, which has the effect of unifying the plots, since all centres on her from now on. She is the pivot of Mirabell's plot and Fainall's designs, with background sparring between Millamant, Mrs Marwood and Mrs Fainall as the spice of revelation. Act 4 is largely balanced between Sir Wilfull and Sir Rowland; Act 5 produces the final unravelling. Dramatic tension is slight until that last act, but the symmetry of the whole makes it an aesthetically pleasing play.

Style

Hazlitt's quotation, a definition of the effects of Congreve's style, has already been given in the section on *The author and his work*. The term 'wit' in the seventeenth century covered several different modes of expression and standards of behaviour, among them truth to nature, the mature application of judgement, flights of fancy or imagination and the use of similitudes. Wit in the Restoration period was often antisocial or sexually free in its emphasis, whereas by the time Joseph Addison (1672–1719) came to contribute his papers to *The Spectator* (1711) the tone had become distinctly moral.

Hobbes saw wit as embracing both fancy and judgement together, or at the least partaking of one or the other. Frequently vivacity and sophistication were involved, and intellectual perception (or superiority) was of the essence; images and ideas could thus be happily blended in the appropriate form.

By the time Congreve was writing in the early 1690s, true wit was concerned with decorum or judgement; and the ability to 'turn a phrase' was highly valued in poetry and prose alike. Congreve believed that the true wit of his play would exercise decorum and judgement, and that the Witwoud-type character is therefore a kind of buffoon since he is lacking in both. Raillery, polite jesting and sometimes satire are parts of wit, as is the invention of similitudes, upon which most of Witwoud's speech depends. Fujimura, in *The Restoration Comedy of Wit*, defines the difference between true and false wit: 'In true wit the dominant ideal is that of decorum, there is no forced comparison and no excess, and consequently the latter, puns and bawdy references belong to the lower domain of false wit.' The poet Cowley further suggested that false wit had no individual life of its own. Quibbling, paradox, antithesis were also regarded by critics of the day as false wit. The double-entendre, frequently with sexual implications, is also a mode of false wit, since it is dependent on 'forced' word-play. It will be seen from all this that Congreve employs both true and false wit, through Mirabell and Millamant on the one hand and Petulant and Witwoud on the other. In addition, what George Meredith (1828–1909) asserted was the 'flow of boudoir Billingsgate in Lady Wishfort [being] unmatched for the vigour and pointedness of the tongue', is, though false wit, underpinned by what Bonamy Dobrée rightly noted as a brilliant choice of vowel sounds.

Witwoud lacks decorum because his commonplace-book addiction means that false comparisons flow from him in an untapped rush and also because, like Petulant, he is at times on the edge of farce. Witwoud's type is forever captured in the Duke of Buckingham's couplet:

> Not quite so low as fool, nor quite a top,
> But hangs between 'em both, and is a fop.

For, as Dennis observed, 'He who has wit without judgement is but a half wit.'

A 'true wit' like Mirabell has judgement and learning, as we see from his literary references as well as those of Millamant. Fujimura admirably sums up his own writings on the nature of wit when he says that 'Wit is a very comprehensive and ambiguous term, and it is sometimes contradictory in its implications: as judgement it implies restraint, good taste, common sense and naturalness; as fancy, on the other hand, it implies whatever is novel and striking and remote.' The foregoing may be seen as an overture to the movements of Congreve's masterly verbal symphony; far from having what a critic called 'a brilliant and soulless art', Congreve is a stylist at once learned and, on occasion, coarse (though here not to be compared with Wycherley), the exponent of true wit as a moral measure and false wit as a character limitation. He is the maker of epigrams, the coiner of repartee, and much more than the 'professional funny man' which John L. Palmer, the novelist and dramatic critic (1885–1944), would have us believe he is. He was prudent in his life, wise in his choice of friends, hence a true wit in his life as well as in his writing, observing what Lady Wishfort would call 'decorums' but without the stain of her scarcely-concealed motives.

Congreve was a scholar and critic of no mean order, and consequently *The Way of the World* has what we might call a dual sub-text; the first part of this is characterized by the learning and wisdom that sustain the play, the second by the unvoiced morality that runs through it. Any writer who studies Restoration Comedy sooner or later finds himself in one of two critical camps. Either he sees the reflection of a moral code in the plays, or he sees merely the record of libertine situations and innuendo. Undoubtedly Congreve is a moralist, subscribing to the humour of the time (but remember that it is the time of William and Mary, and thus of reaction against Restoration excesses); yet throughout the play he mocks the predilections of fashionable society, and points the way to true decorum and a way of life independent of tinsel language or emotional indulgence. Consequently, his intentions are revealed as serious; Witwoud lives, as so many lived at the time, believing that effect and ostentation are the measures of living. Petulant follows in similar style, but it is a mimic dance, not life. Fainall and Mrs Fainall have married without scruples, he in order to get her estate while she, initially taken with him, is saved only by the moral responsibility of Mirabell, who has her estate made over to him and restores it to her at the opportune moment. Admittedly, this could be seen as part of his amoral manipulation of Lady Wishfort; but the moral index to Mirabell and Millamant is their cool exchanges of independence, their recognition of integrity and individuality, contrasting with the cynical way of the world that circumscribes the lives and motives of the other characters.

Beneath Congreve's wit there is a sombre and unpleasant recognition of greed, lust, licentiousness, perhaps best epitomized by Fainall and Mrs Marwood, and it is noteworthy that Mirabell has to play them at their own game in order to defeat them. Congreve admirably defines his main concerns in the play in his otherwise sycophantic dedication to Ralph, Earl of Montague. He writes of being moved to 'design some characters which should appear ridiculous, not so much through a natural folly (which is incorrigible, and therefore not proper for the stage) as through an affected wit; a wit which, at the same time that it is affected is also false'. He goes on to castigate those critics who, he says, having seen *The Way of the World* still found difficulty in distinguishing 'betwixt the character of a Witwoud and a Truewit'. Defective wit is thus exposed in the play, but at the time this did not make for an active audience appreciation. The allusions were, of course, educated ones (Suckling and Waller are quoted, and even Sir Wilfull mentions Pylades and Orestes), and there is a fine balance of phraseology and subtlety of thought throughout.

Repartee is central to the movement of the play, particularly where Mirabell is involved with either Millamant, Fainall, or Witwoud. The celebrated 'proviso' scene shows the wit of Mirabell and Millamant at its best; Mirabell actually thinks ahead to fatherhood (inconceivable in earlier Restoration comedy), insisting that Millamant shall not go in for lacing 'till you mould my boy's head like a sugar-loaf; and instead of a man-child, make me father to a crooked-billet'. Millamant's wit is perhaps more whimsical than Mirabell's. Although the 'proviso' scene reflects her real thoughts as well as her 'act' before society, her first entrance shows her in masterly form in the exchanges with Mincing: 'I am persecuted with letters – I hate letters – nobody knows how to write letters; and yet one has 'em, one does not know why. – They serve one to pin up one's hair'. She extends this fancy with delightful affectation, abetted by Mincing, into the idea that only letters written in the form of poetry will make the proper curl-papers for her hair. She subscribes to the 'truewit' values, for she has judgement and culture; she despises the illiterate and boorish and scorns the effusions of Witwoud and Petulant.

The song beginning, "Tis not to wound a wanton boy' is further testimony to Millamant's wit, for the judgement she exercises here is designed to humiliate Mrs Marwood, who aspires to be Mirabell's mistress (and who therefore 'sighed in vain'). Not so Millamant, who can command Mirabell if she wishes.

As we see in the section on *Characters* all those in the play represent a considerable development of the prototypes on which they are based. Fainall is flawed and therefore cannot be a truewit, for he has both mercenary and libertine predilections. His mistress Mrs Marwood has considerable intellect and judgement, yet is tainted by her own licence and the nature of her subterfuge. Sir Wilfull appears to be a boor, but has the judgement to be right-thinking and witty too when the occasion demands, as he proves in his 'bear-garden' riposte to Fainall. Lady Wishfort's humour varies between the coarse but strikingly self-honest ('I look like an old peeled wall'), and her own ridiculous affectations, with their sexual repressions finding an unconscious verbal release ('If you think the least scruple of carnality was an ingredient').

The many manifestations of wit include irony, frequently with an antithetical balance ('You have a taste extremely delicate, and are for refining on your pleasures'). There is a superb range of reference: tightly economical; sometimes with a nice tinge of malice ('where they come together like the coroner's inquest to sit upon the murdered reputations of the week'). There are fine coinages, sometimes with political innuendo ('Cabal-nights'). There is irony in town, poets, and fashion, with both learned and contemporary reference ('he's as loving as the monster in *The Tempest*'), and some natural imagery to underpin the limitations of the natural: 'like a medlar grafted on a crab' (i.e. on a crab-apple). Congreve employs satire against contemporary poets and the pedantry of literary fashion ('as heavy as a panegyric in a funeral sermon, or a copy of commendatory verses from one poet to another'). Punning runs throughout, usually with a sexual double-entendre ('the more opportunities to show his natural parts'). And there is humour of situation (Witwoud's account of 'two fasting strumpets and a bawd troubled with wind') which, he says, is a set-up by Petulant to create an impression of his own reputation with the ladies. Petulant himself has certain bluntly epigrammatic turns ('Anger helps complexion, saves paint').

The range of Congreve's satire is considerable, some of it coming via Witwoud's similitudes ('she hates Mirabell worse than a quaker hates a parrot'). Falseness and artificiality of manner or standards are forever pilloried in Mirabell's pungent line 'To save that idol reputation'; and satire is inlaid with situation comedy, since Mirabell's plot with his pretended uncle underlines that falseness of appearances which enables Lady Wishfort to be mercilessly satirized for what Sir John Betjeman would have called her 'late-flowering lust'. Congreve also has a fine ear; witness his capturing of Mincing's affectations: 'But when your laship pins it up with poetry, it sits so pleasant the next day as anything, and is so pure and so crips'; or the way in which Waitwell claims (as husband) his right to the money which Foible receives for her services to Mirabell.

The tendency to use French terms, a kind of fashionable verbal monogram, is also satirized (Beaumonde, deshabille). Arranged marriages in which husband and wife grow apart according to the convention, and keep apart in order to make a reputation, are kept under constant harassment by Congreve, the couplets at the end of each act commenting in some way on the marriage state. In fact Congreve's range is fashion and society itself, from Puritan references to Prynne and Quarles, pregnant ladies or the hanging of thieves at Tyburn.

General questions and sample answer in note form

1 What are the main aspects of Congreve's style in *The Way of the World*?
2 Write an essay on the differences between a wit and a truewit, referring closely to two of the characters in the play.
3 Discuss and illustrate Congreve's use of contrast in *The Way of the World*.
4 What do you learn of fashionable society of the time in *The Way of the World*. Refer to the text in support of your views.
5 Write a character study of Mirabell, and say what he contributes to the plot of the play.
6 Write an essay on Congreve's treatment of *marriage* in *The Way of the World*.
7 Compare and contrast the characters of Lady Wishfort and Sir Wilfull Witwoud.
8 Estimate the part played by Witwoud in the play.
9 In what ways is Millamant an attractive heroine? You should refer closely to the text in your answer.
10 Do you think that Congreve is a moral writer? Give reasons for your answer by reference to the play.
11 Write an essay on the parts played by Mrs Marwood and Fainall in the play.
12 'The plot is needlessly complex.' How far would you agree with this statement?
13 Write an appreciation of the role taken by the various servants in the play.
14 'Delightful to read, boring to see staged.' How far would you agree with this assessment of *The Way of the World*?
15 Write an essay on the *coarseness* in *The Way of the World*.

Suggested notes for essay answer to question 1

(a) *Introduction* – one paragraph on the nature of Restoration comedy as evidenced by *The Way of the World*. Word-play, fashion, society, affectation, etc. should be included, with reference either just to Congreve or to another dramatist.

(b) Wit and judgement or decorum (quote – perhaps from Mirabell or Millamant). Mockery, joking, satire (of society or convention, etc.) – quote. Emphasize by reference to true wit and decorum as major aspects of Congreve's style.

(c) Congreve's use of false wit – puns (though these vary) – bawdy references and innuendoes – quibbles, paradox, antithesis (quote) – *double entendre* (often sexual). Refer to use of contrasting wit or false wit in particular characters.

(d) Epigrams, repartee, swiftness of the repartee in particular. Quote to indicate *pace* of dialogue – wit as moral measure – learning – wisdom – exposure of greed and the nature of society in which he lives.

(e) Allusions, contemporary references – the 'proviso' scene as evidence of wit – the dual levels of superficiality and seriousness on which Congreve shows his verbal dexterity. Use of song (' 'Tis not to wound a wanton boy') – degrees of irony – even to self-honesty ('I look like an old peeled wall').

Conclusion – The sheer range of the satire, political references, French terms, marriages, etc. Choose what you think are the most important and sophisticated of Congreve's effects, and quote briefly in support of them.

Further reading

A Preface to Restoration Drama, John Harold Wilson (Harvard University Press)
Lectures on the English Comic Writers, William Hazlitt (Everyman's Library)
Essays in Critical Dissent, F. W. Bateson (Longman)

Brodie's Notes

TITLES IN THE SERIES

Edward Albee	Who's Afraid of Virginia Woolf?
Jane Austen	Emma
Jane Austen	Mansfield Park
Jane Austen	Pride and Prejudice
Samuel Beckett	Waiting for Godot
William Blake	Songs of Innocence and Experience
Robert Bolt	A Man for All Seasons
Charlotte Brontë	Jane Eyre
Emily Brontë	Wuthering Heights
Geoffrey Chaucer	The Franklin's Tale
Geoffrey Chaucer	The Knight's Tale
Geoffrey Chaucer	The Miller's Tale
Geoffrey Chaucer	The Nun's Priest's Tale
Geoffrey Chaucer	The Pardoner's Prologue and Tale
Geoffrey Chaucer	Prologue to the Canterbury Tales
Geoffrey Chaucer	The Wife of Bath's Tale
Wilkie Collins	Woman in White
Joseph Conrad	Heart of Darkness
Charles Dickens	Great Expectations
Charles Dickens	Hard Times
Charles Dickens	Oliver Twist
Charles Dickens	A Tale of Two Cities
Gerald Durrell	My Family and Other Animals
George Eliot	Silas Marner
T. S. Eliot	Selected Poems
Henry Fielding	Tom Jones
F. Scott Fitzgerald	The Great Gatsby and Tender is the Night
E. M. Forster	Howard's End
E. M. Forster	A Passage to India
John Fowles	The French Lieutenant's Woman
Anne Frank	The Diary of Anne Frank
Mrs Gaskell	North and South
William Golding	Lord of the Flies
Graham Greene	Brighton Rock
Graham Greene	The Power and the Glory
Graham Handley (ed)	The Metaphysical Poets: John Donne to Henry Vaughan
Thomas Hardy	Far From the Madding Crowd
Thomas Hardy	The Mayor of Casterbridge
Thomas Hardy	The Return of the Native
Thomas Hardy	Tess of the D'Urbervilles
L. P. Hartley	The Go-Between
Aldous Huxley	Brave New World
James Joyce	Portrait of the Artist as a Young Man
John Keats	Selected Poems and Letters of John Keats
Philip Larkin	Selected Poems of Philip Larkin

D. H. Lawrence	**The Rainbow**
D. H. Lawrence	**Sons and Lovers**
D. H. Lawrence	**Women in Love**
Harper Lee	**To Kill a Mockingbird**
Laurie Lee	**Cider with Rosie**
Christopher Marlowe	**Dr Faustus**
Arthur Miller	**The Crucible**
Arthur Miller	**Death of a Salesman**
John Milton	**Paradise Lost**
Robert C. O'Brien	**Z for Zachariah**
Sean O'Casey	**Juno and the Paycock**
George Orwell	**Animal Farm**
George Orwell	**1984**
J. B. Priestley	**An Inspector Calls**
J. D. Salinger	**The Catcher in the Rye**
William Shakespeare	**Antony and Cleopatra**
William Shakespeare	**As You Like It**
William Shakespeare	**Hamlet**
William Shakespeare	**Henry IV Part I**
William Shakespeare	**Julius Caesar**
William Shakespeare	**King Lear**
William Shakespeare	**Macbeth**
William Shakespeare	**Measure for Measure**
William Shakespeare	**The Merchant of Venice**
William Shakespeare	**A Midsummer Night's Dream**
William Shakespeare	**Much Ado about Nothing**
William Shakespeare	**Othello**
William Shakespeare	**Richard II**
William Shakespeare	**Romeo and Juliet**
William Shakespeare	**The Tempest**
William Shakespeare	**Twelfth Night**
George Bernard Shaw	**Pygmalion**
Alan Sillitoe	**Selected Fiction**
John Steinbeck	**Of Mice and Men** and **The Pearl**
Jonathan Swift	**Gulliver's Travels**
Dylan Thomas	**Under Milk Wood**
Alice Walker	**The Color Purple**
W. B. Yeats	**Selected Poetry**

ENGLISH COURSEWORK BOOKS

Terri Apter	**Women and Society**
Kevin Dowling	**Drama and Poetry**
Philip Gooden	**Conflict**
Philip Gooden	**Science Fiction**
Margaret K. Gray	**Modern Drama**
Graham Handley	**Modern Poetry**
Graham Handley	**Prose**
Graham Handley	**Childhood and Adolescence**
R. J. Sims	**The Short Story**